Also by Ruby Gwin

A Day That Would End Tearing at Your Heart

The 250th Field Artillery Men Remember World War II

World War II

Walter Irvin's Diary: World War I Pharmacist Mate

1st Lt. Raymond Miller Pilot

Colonel (Ret.) Harry G. Canham

Humble and Gentle in Victory Pilot's Courage,
Faith and Patriotism
1942-1974

Ruby Gwin

Order this book online at www.trafford.com
or email orders@trafford.com

Most Trafford titles are also available at major online book retailers.

© Copyright 2015 Ruby Gwin.
Cover design: Ruby Gwin
Book design: Ruby Gwin

Print information available on the last page.

ISBN: 978-1-4907-6624-9 (sc)
ISBN: 978-1-4907-6623-2 (hc)
ISBN: 978-1-4907-6625-6 (e)

Library of Congress Control Number: 2015917982

Because of the dynamic nature of the Internet, any web addresses or links contained in
this book may have changed since publication and may no longer be valid. The views
expressed in this work are solely those of the author and do not necessarily reflect the
views of the publisher, and the publisher hereby disclaims any responsibility for them.

Any people depicted in stock imagery provided by Thinkstock are models,
and such images are being used for illustrative purposes only.
Certain stock imagery © Thinkstock.

Trafford rev. 1/08/2016

 www.trafford.com
North America & international
toll-free: 1 888 232 4444 (USA & Canada)
fax: 812 355 4082

Contents

To all the AC-130 members lost in combat, and the ones, including maintenance men, who bravely served and returned.

Acknowledgments

Most and above all, special thanks to retired Col. Harry Canham, a distinguished flying pilot, for his candid account of his military operations, flying across the skies in war- and peacetime to *defeat* and *protect*. Thanks to Harry's wife, Carlyn, for her invaluable contribution, because she took a leading role in gathering information that helped shape the book into what it is. Carlyn was forthcoming and informative helping with details, articles, pictures, and enthusiasm. Special thanks to Harry's son, Michael, for his helpful input. The passage of time for Michael *never* diminished, recalling some humorous stories of his father's military encounters—especially in Africa. Also, special thanks to Michelle Canham Sergel for copies of her keepsake mementoes of her loving Granddaddy's air force days. It has been an incredible journey working with Colonel Canham, Carlyn, Michael, and Michelle.

Thanks to Harry's niece and nephew, Elizabeth Canham Johnson and James "Jim" Canham, who shared pictures and information for their Uncle Harry's story. Also invaluable were personal pictures and mission stories by flight engineer Sgt. Billy D. Gilmore and daughter, Kamiah Gilmore Hove. I found all the contributions invaluable and want to express my sincere thanks to each.

To my *special* publishing team at Trafford Publishing for their contributions in seeing that every little detail is taken care of. To each—a heartfelt thanks: Heidi Morgan, check-in coordinator; Yza Gomez, publishing consultant; Jodie Lambert, senior marketing consultant; Dave Walters, publishing supervisor; John Cain, marketing service representative; Steven Lancin, senior book sales consultant; and Leslie Tan, marketing services representative.

Introduction

It has been seventy-two years since retired USAF Col. Harry G. Canham, SN 40475A, entered the Army Air Corps in 1942. He flew combat missions during World War II and Vietnam, peacetime, and was awarded five Distinguished Flying Crosses (heroism) while participating in aerial flights in Vietnam. As in every area in his life, Harry G. Canham used his skills to enhance those around him; he never tried to draw attention to himself.

Harry Canham was working to attain a higher education in 1941 when Pearl Harbor was attacked on 7 December 1941. The overrunning of Europe by Nazi Germany and the Japanese attack on the United States Pacific Fleet's base Pearl Harbor, Hawaii, jolted the United States into the most widespread war in history. At the outset of World War II, the United States had no plans to get into conflict with any nation, but then knowing that Japan was bent on war, the United States had no choice but to declare war on Japan. The war would become more universal.

It was clear to Harry Canham and his high school friends that their country needed help for the survival of the country. They chose to volunteer. Wanting to fly, Harry joined the Army Air Corps. He served his country until his retirement in March 1974 with thirty-two years active duty and active reserves.

In Vietnam, Harry was seriously injured and flown back stateside to the United States Air Force Hospital at Scott Air Force Base in St. Clair County, Illinois, where he spent close to five months from 1 August 1967 to 21 December 1967. In the last of December of 1967,

Harry returned to fly eighty-six more missions. During his course of duties, he lived in tents, huts, on and off base. Quoting Union Army general William Tecumseh Sherman during the American Civil War, "War is hell" to which Harry agreed 100 percent and said, "To protect my country, I would go to war as long as I live."

Harry flew the C-124s, the largest aircraft in the United States Air Force and nicknamed Old Shaky by her crew, which was a critical tool for the war. Old Shaky made an immediate impact in Korea and was the backbone of airlift to Vietnam.

Harry earned, plus his Distinguished Flying Crosses, thirty-two flying medals, six Meritorious Service Medals, and two National Defense Service Medals. One was the Vietnamese highest congressional medal for a mission Harry's general had sent him out to do. He saved a group of South Vietnam commander's troops, Angkor Wat, and a community in Central Cambodia on the mission flying the Lockheed AC-130E Gunship, a heavy ground attack aircraft. In the end, the gunships were the crown jewel that inspired Harry the most. The gunship legacies still continue to unfold.

Harry flew missions where his exploits took place away from the spotlight with a quiet resolve to see each job through. He flew the skies experiencing the awfulness of bombing and strafing and carrying nuclear weapons on his gunship without much beforehand warning. Harry would go out, strap in, and take off to protect and defend, flying the skies on top secret missions. The book contains *some* classified missions released in 2000. Some records are not researchable yet, and there are millions of records and government resources that are limited.

Harry also flew the Martin B-26 that offered a level of its crew's operational immunity unmatched by any other aircraft in its class. He served in Vietnam, two tours. He flew assignments from England to Russia, India, North Africa to Cairo, Egypt, etc. Harry was in Korea after World War II for three weeks on assignment.

Col. Harry Canham's story brings to life a pivotal time while honorably serving his country as squadron pilot, trainer, director, and commander as he piloted several models of aircraft on special operations. Harry flew numerous top secret missions during World War II, seventy-six missions in gunships, plus ten missions in F-4 Phantom fighter to protect and defend in Vietnam and eight F-4 flights off a carrier during active reserve and active air force duty. He stayed focused on procedures with determination to do the job and to complete a mission as top priority. Incredible and dangerous, he did his job, flying in the skies albeit knowing he may be looking death in the face. He functioned beyond what was thought of as a brave or heroic capacity. Making a difference was just a part of Harry's DNA.

Hearing of Col. Harry Canham's military service planted the seed for his story. His story offers a window to the mind of the man that is as relevant today as it was at the time of events. Harry had never given thought to relating his story and is very reserved in talking about his combat role in the military. Harry's story is a simplified history of thirty-two years, stories of a pilot; one can participate in some accounts of the dangerous mission that he flew. It is impossible to write all the stories of Harry's heroism, for most of his missions were classified top secret. Fortunately, because of young men as Harry, we are able to live free with liberty today. Those freedoms we cherish yet sometimes take for granted, just as it provides for us, it expects of us. Hopefully, the book will provide for the reader some insight into Colonel Canham's low-profile display. He was always genuine with moral standards, an extraordinarily successful professional pilot turned out by the United States Army Air Forces and United States Air Force. His many honors have never turned his head, and he remains modest with no pompous display.

Colonel Canham's story is as fresh and timely now as when events happened. Harry and the millions of his comrades were just young men who left the comforts of home and family to fight fascism and prevailed militarily with duty, honor, and heroism to bring a dictator to heel. Unfortunately, unless our veterans' stories, memories, and experiences of having triumphed over adversity during a time of monumental loss of life and economic devastation are told and relived, they will soon be lost to history.

Chapter One

A Courageous Decision

This story is a product of 22,000 hours of a veteran pilot's military operations during World War II, Korea, NATO, Vietnam, and peacetime. Col. Harry Canham displayed moral as well as physical courage throughout those many miles. For Harry Canham, no greater honor could come than the opportunity to be an aviator flying the skies to the bitter end in order to restore all that is good and decent and righteous for his country.

Young Harry Canham was working by day and going to night school in 1941. Harry and his friends, after graduating from high school, had to work and hoped to achieve a higher education working in factories or on farms. During the day, Harry worked surface mining or, as some called it, strip mining, where first, a long strip of overlying soil and rock (the overburden) is removed to mine the coal. Large machines are used in this type of mining. An operator of heavy equipment had to have a special permit. Harry operated a dragline moving the ore body to be excavated that lay relatively near the surface. He also drove a twenty-five-ton coal truck. Harry said driving the coal truck was anything but fun. The only time you stopped the truck was where you were loading down in the pit. When you'd go across the hopper, you'd slow down and dump out the bottom and make a U-turn and go back to the pit, put your foot on the carburetor, and go. The country was just starting to recover from the Great Depression. Harry knew a college education would be a great plus for his future plans.

Harry was born on 3 September 1920, in the northern part of Illinois, in the small town of Wataga, with a population of five hundred people. It was in Wataga where Harry grew up and went to school. His class graduated seventeen in 1938.

Harry was the son of Albert and Opal Canham. He had one sister named Ruth and one brother, Morris H., "Jim." His brother was attending the University of Illinois, studying mechanical engineering, when war broke out. On 20 September 1943, Morris volunteered for the Army Air Corps and went to gunnery school. He served in the European theater as a tail gunner in B-26s and A-26s. He also served as an aerial gunnery instructor 2554. Morris's wish was also to be a pilot, but his health stopped those wishes. He was five years older than Harry.

Harry's father worked for the railroad as an agent and telegraph operator (Morse code) in a little town outside of Wataga, Illinois, which was a big hub for CMQ. He'd put the trains on the right track to go into Chicago. There was a lot of freight traffic during the war. People returned to the rails due to the new streamliner concept, and the government needed the trains to move a large number of troops. Without the railroads, World War II certainly could not have been won. Albert worked seven days a week his whole life without a day off. He retired at age seventy-two.

Harry's father taught him to telegraph. Harry would go in and help his father on weekends especially in wintertime; when it was snowing the tracks would cut and throw switches off. The fellows that had to clean the tracks couldn't come in and help his father. When the weather turned good, they'd come in and help. When they had not much to do, Albert would put Harry over at the telegraph, and when he got where he could receive a telegraph coming in, his father told Harry to get it, for he didn't have the time. It helped his father, for there was no one else that could do his job. His father was an excellent teacher and a practical railroader. Later, those telegraph teachings of his father's would be beneficial for the decision Harry would make.

Harry always enjoyed hunting and was out hunting one day in 1941 and had gotten a raccoon. A black fella came up and told him he'd better put his dogs in the car for a fella was going to take them. Harry put them in the car and was sitting there, talking with the black fella. The black fella said, "What are you going to do with the raccoon?" Harry said, "I'll skin it and sell the skin." The black fella told Harry that he would skin the raccoon and put the skin on a board and everything for the meat, which was all right with Harry. The black fella invited Harry over for dinner, and he went. Harry said, "I had a nice dinner and ate my first taste of raccoon. It was a beginning of a good friendship."

Harry and two school friends had gone quail hunting on 7 December 1941; unbeknownst to them, the day would change their day of hunting when they went to Shorty Woolsey's little country store for a sandwich and milk. There weren't restaurants as we have today. It was while eating that they learned about the attack on Pearl Harbor. Most people at that time learned the news by word of mouth or heard it on the radio. The Japanese imperial forces had launched a surprise attack on the United States naval base at Pearl Harbor, Hawaii.

Things seemed to unfold quickly on 8 December 1941—the United States and Britain declared war on Japan; on 11 December 1941, Germany and Italy declared war on the United States, and on 25 December 1941, Hong Kong surrendered to Japan. There was no question left for America but answer back. The Japanese attack inevitably led to a cataclysmic global nightmare; it was quite clear to Harry and his high school friends that their country needed them. Harry and his two friends, as many other young men, never waited to receive an official-looking postcard of a presidential draft notice. In 1942, Harry and his friends went to the selective service board and volunteered, each as individuals chose to go to the Army Air Corps. The number of volunteers was enormous for the flying/aviation cadet pilot training program. They were at a young age, athletic, and displayed integrity. Leaving home was not that difficult for Harry because he wanted to fly. Aviation had always been his passion.

There was a locally owned airport in nearby Galesburg, Illinois, that had Civil Air Patrol. Harry with his two friends went out to the airport and took a written paper test to fly. The privately owned airport needed help, so Harry and his friends worked between flights, showing the airplanes around, putting in fuel and oil, and checking the tires. One day, the owner came down and told Harry to get in and that they were going flying. Before long, he had Harry to go solo and fly around. He went with Harry a couple of times and then sent Harry out in the area to fly. While working at the airport, Harry was checked out in a light aircraft before entering the military in 1942.

The light aircraft used at the Galesburg, Illinois, airport was the same as the Army Air Corps used to train glider pilots. Harry and his two friends thought they were getting in as power training aviation cadets—not so! Harry was sent to glider school in Billings, Texas. One of his friends was sent to Mississippi. After Harry and his friend got through that training they found out the upper class had a 100 percent loss. They were staff sergeants. Those of age could go to power training if they could meet all requirements but would lose out as staff sergeants and go back to private if they were washed out of power training.

Allied combined with bomber offensive began its aerial war phase against Germany in 1943. Meanwhile, Harry is in cadet training. The long road of Pearl Harbor—it was clear for conduct of warfare to be effective it was important for the military to increased time on their training, preparation, and logistics. Harry had no idea what military life would be like. To accomplish being a pilot, Harry knew he must not only act or plan but also believe. The Army Air Corps training would be grueling and competitive it must meet Army Air Corps weight and physical conditioning with good eye requirements. Candidates must be dedicated to achieving excellence and accountability of all required programs. They must have the knowledge to absorb and view all the technical data along with an inner vision with state of mind. They must be highly confident, professional, and sharp to meet the demands of an air force pilot's career. For Harry, there was no quitting or lack of courage; that was a given. "Military school was tough," Harry said. "However, I learned to respect the schools, and today I am very thankful."

The USAAF pilot schools were first primary flying training, where cadets are taught basic flight training using a two-seater training aircraft. The day finally came for which Harry had waited, and each cadet was given sixty hours of flight training for nine weeks before moving on to basic flight school. Basic flying training taught the cadets to fly in formation, fly by instrument or by aerial navigation, fly at night, and fly long distances. A cadet had to have about seventy flight hours training in the North American BT-9, a low-wing single-piston engine monoplane primary trainer aircraft, and Vultee BT-13 Valiant, which was an American World War-era basic trainer. Harry found flying over Galesburg, Illinois, was much different from the maneuvers that were performed in the military. Each airplane was used in the second phase of the three-phase training program for cadets before being promoted to advance training. Advanced flying training placed the graduate in two categories: single-engine and multiengine. Harry flew the single-engine North American Aviation AT-6C Texan, the AT-6D Texan advanced trainer, and the United States Army Air Forces multiengine Beechcraft AT-11 Kansan advanced bombing trainer. Cadets were supposed to get a total of seventy-five to eighty flight hours before graduating and getting their pilots wings, and the transition pilot training single-engine pilots transitioned to fighters and fighter-bombers and multiengine pilots transitioned to transport or bombers. Harry flew bombers, but he mainly transited to piloting transport.

When Harry got in military pilot school in Sherman, Texas, the class was told that if anybody could telegraph in seven to eight words a minute, they could be let out of class. With that, Harry took the challenge, for he had been taught Morse code by his father. The fellow told him to get himself over there, sit down, and they will see. Harry didn't know what the fellow had set the machine at, but he was taking it going as fast as he could. When the test was done, the fellow told Harry to get out of there.

Harry said, "I think I did seven." The fellow responded, "Thirty-five words a minute, that is what I set the machine on." The average is twenty-five words per minute.

Harry had two years of college. There was mathematics that he hadn't had. He had some of it, but not all of it. Harry said, "That gave him time to study mathematics—that is what got me through."

The aerial war moved into critical phase in 1943; it would be the beginning of the Allies's Combined Bomber Offense against Germany. Late 1943, Harry was given the opportunity to enter the Aviation Cadet Flying Program (School) in Waco, Texas, to learn to fly powered aircraft. It was the first basic flying training school to become operational after Pearl Harbor on 7 December 1941. The base would later be changed to Colonel Connelly Air Force Base. Colonel Connelly was killed in Japan in 1945.

Deaths for the United States Army Air Forces were one-third to training. Cadets who graduated at the top of their class were graded as second lieutenants. Harry graduated from that school with his wings and was commissioned second lieutenant. For Harry, it was a great day on 5 December 1943, a defining time, for he was fulfilling his dream to fly. "Of my cadet experience," Harry said, "I missed my family and friends, but I soon found new *lifetime* friends who were also missing their family and friends."

A one-dollar short snorter bill everyone from flight school decorated with signatures during early 1942. Upon receiving their wings and commissioned as second lieutenant to fly, each left with one signed by all the others. The inscribed bill served as a good luck token. A piece of World War II history flew with Harry on every mission during the war.

Chapter Two

North Africa Assignment

In 1944, Harry was sent to Dodge City, Kansas, for Martin B-26 school and from there to RTU (Replacement Training Unit) in Lake Charles, Louisiana, which was renamed Chennault Air Force Base after Gen. Claire Lee Chennault and his acclaimed F-40 Flying Aces, an American Volunteers Group (1941–1942). The Flying Tigers pilots comprised of three groups of USAA Corps, Navy, and Marine Corps. They combated Japanese bombing raids on China, and the Chinese people continue to honor the general and say, "He saved our country."

The dozen B-26 airplanes delivered to Dodge City Army Air Field were the first B-26s to be used for instruction. It was very essential that each pilot and crew member thoroughly familiarize himself with the plane and its operation system in order to accomplish intended missions. Standard procedure landings and takeoff instructions for the B-26 were used. Discretion was left to the pilot as to what action to take and when necessary.

Before takeoff, the pilots and crew performed a rigorous check of the aircraft testing all instruments, flight controls, and equipment. The Martin B-26 Marauder was World War II's most controversial aircraft. It was built with a high-speed range; it was not an aircraft for low-level attack, where high-level strategic missions were more successful. The aircraft wings had no visible means of support. On final runway approach and when the engine was out, the aircraft had to be flown at exact airspeed; this was intimidating to inexperienced pilots who were used to flying at much slower speeds. Whenever they'd slowed down below what the manual stated, the aircraft would stall and crash. Trainees stateside (at home) had a series of training accidents, causing the aircraft to earn nicknames such as the Widow-Maker. The USAAF, concerned about the high accident rate, seriously considered withdrawing the Marauder from production and service.

The Martin B-26 Marauder, it turned out, could be safely flown *if* the crews were sufficiently trained. After an investigation into the problem, it was found there was *no* reason why the aircraft should be discontinued. Veteran pilots in combat overseas had enough experience that they could handle the high speed. It was thought it could not be flown on one engine. Experienced pilots, including Jimmy Doolittle, proved the merits of the bomber by proving it could be flown on one engine. The problems were traced to the inexperience of both aircrew and ground crews and overloading of the aircraft. After aerodynamic and design change and crew training, the Marauder offered a level of operational immunity to its crews, unmatched by any other aircraft in its class. It was the first Allied bomber in the European theater or war to fly two hundred operational missions. The B-26 was the first aircraft to test the bicycle-type landing gear that would later be adopted for use by the air force on the B-47 and B-52 jet bombers. The bomber from medium altitude proved to be a highly accurate bomber. The Ninth Air Force would prove the Martin B-26 Marauder's high-level strategic missions' true capability to be most successful. Its record ended the war with the lowest loss rate per thousand sorties of any light bomber used in the European theater.

Air warfare was the principal component used in all theaters during World War II and, simultaneous with anti-air attacks, a large fraction of the industrial output of major powers. Germany and Japan depended on air forces that were closely integrated with land and naval forces and minimized the use of fleets of strategic bombing. At the same time, United States and Britain took the approach of emphasizing strategic bombing and, to a smaller extent, tactical control of the battlefield by air and air defenses. They built a strategic force of large long-range bombers that could carry the air war directly to the enemy's homeland. They built tactical air forces that could win air superiority over the battlefields and, by that, gave vital assistance to ground troops. As did Japan, a powerful naval-air component was built based on aircraft carriers, which played the central role in the war at sea.

Harry flew several aircraft overseas, England, India, etc. He was assigned to fly the B-26 Marauder and ferried B-26 aircraft to England by the way of North Africa. In 1945 to 1946, Harry was assigned to North Africa. He ferried both models of the Martin B-26B Marauder and the B-26G Marauder; actually, he flew all the B-26 models. He was in North Africa for one year and three months and ended up in Cairo, Egypt.

While ferrying B-26s, Harry stopped for crew rest on the south side of the Amazon River. Harry was located in a crude building on a cot, asleep, when a monkey jumped on him and scared him to death. He opened the window, and the monkey jump out as frightened as Harry. The Amazon rain forest, also known as the Amazon jungle, is the world's largest ecosystems, containing one of the most diverse arrays of species on Earth. There are numerous species of monkeys in the tropical rain forest.

On one of several ferrying trips to England by way of North Africa, a young native employed at the base would always meet Harry and take care of him on his stop at the air base. Harry wore leather boots, which the young boy always admired. The boy had never had a pair of shoes, let alone a pair of boots. Harry didn't know what to get the boy and decided the next time he came down through South America, he'd buy the biggest pair of leather boots they had available for the young lad. Harry said, "When I gave him the boots, the boy came back in about thirty minutes wearing them. He was real proud of those leather boots."

The young African boy made the beds, cleaned the rooms, and got water for four or five rooms. He lived on base to work. All the bases in Africa were small with small runways. There were just a few places to stay with a mess hall. The boy was in his late teens or early twenties—for Harry it was hard to tell. The boy spoke some English.

The boy invited Harry home with him. The base commander said to Harry, "Why don't you take him out where he lives so he can show the boots to his family. I'll get you a jeep." Harry said, "I don't want to get out there and get lost." The commander said, "I don't think you will get lost, just go out there and back. I will send a couple of extra five-gallon cans of gas, but I don't think you will need it."

So Harry took the jeep and drove the boy home. It was twenty-seven miles. Harry said, "Everything was fine . . . just nobody wore any clothes. I wasn't sure I was in the right place. The entire family was nude. The boy wore clothes only because of his job at the base. They lived in a mud hut. It wasn't too bad, better than a tent. The huts are cool in the summer and warm in rainy weather."

They invited Harry to eat with them, but he declined. Harry said, "I didn't have time to get sick." The boy's family was very nice to Harry, and the boy wanted to pay for the boots. Of course, Harry said no.

Harry saw the boy several more times, and he was always wearing the boots, just like Harry's. Harry said, "It was the best gift and most rewarding that I ever gave. The experience was one of a few in my career."

Harry and his copilot flew into another similar small air station in Africa, and the copilot went in the bathroom to clean up and shave; he took out his false teeth and laid them down. Harry said, "There was a young black boy in the room that saw the copilot take his teeth out and was standing over, trying to take out his teeth. I told the copilot to put his teeth in his mouth and get out of the bathroom and that I didn't want to go through that again! The young boy was still working on his teeth when I went to bed. The boy must have figured, if that guy took out his teeth, I can take mine out. The boy was all right the next day; he must have decided they won't go."

During Harry's assignment in Africa, he lived in tents and huts. There was a lot of malaria-carrying mosquitoes, and at night, they'd get in bed, pull the sheet up (bug sheet) around them, and spray insecticides, killing the mosquitoes. Harry didn't get a lot of the infections they had over there, saying, "I was lucky, but I sure got sunburned."

Harry experienced much during his stay in Africa. It wasn't easy to see the young live in substandard living, being compounded by families being financially strapped with income at or below poverty level. The poverty level caused a lack of proper education and medical care for Africa's people. Harry later would know how harmful the African sun exposure could be. On his face, arms, and back, his dermatologist went through the alphabet twice, numbering each cancer procedure. The first dermatologist, Dr. Jenson said, "You know, if I didn't know better, I would think you have been in Africa because people from Africa have this same stuff."

Harry responded, "Well, you are looking at one that has been over there for about two years. A lot of it was war. They wanted us over there to send to the Pacific."

Dr. Jenson and Dr. Matthew Kagy, dermatologists, did all Dr. Frederick Mohs's procedures on Harry. Plastic surgeon Dr. Bower had to make a nostril on the left side of Harry's nose so he could breathe. He used Dr. Frederick Mohs's micrographic surgical technique to do the surgery, which is now the most precise and effective way to treat skin cancer that Mohs achieved in 1930. Doctors have adapted new versions of the technique. The excision of a cancer from the skin is followed by the detailed mapping and complete microscope examination of the cancerous tissue and the margins surrounding it. Repeatedly tissue is removed until the margins of the final examine are clear of cancer.

Dr. Bower did a magnificent job. He was able to go in the cheek crease area on the left side of Harry's face and drew it around in place, making a nostril for Harry to breath. It was thought that the surgeon may have to take skin from Harry's stomach. After the surgery, the first thing Harry did was to check his stomach. The nurse told him, "No, we got it from the cheek. The surgeon didn't have to use any skin from the stomach."

Harry had no bruising or any stitches that could be seen after the surgery was over. There were no complications. Mohs surgery eliminates the guesswork in the removal of skin cancers and pinpoints the cancer's location when it is invisible to the naked eye. Presently one in five skin cancers are treated with Mohs surgery. It is a precise, tissue-sparing technique; it provides the highest cure rate with the smallest loss of skin. The cure rate is 99 percent for most cancers, considerably higher than that of other methods used.

Chapter Three

Lost Clothing, ID, and Money

For two years, Harry would start on the east side and fly all across and end up in Egypt. It was after World War II in Europe, and the officials wanted them in Egypt to send to the Pacific. One day, the colonel asked Captain Canham to do him a favor. He wanted Harry to take King Farouk of Egypt wherever he wanted to go. His airplane was down. The king went hunting with Harry and invited him to the palace to see all his collections of guns, etc.

King Farouk lived a glamorous lifestyle. Harry said the women surrounding him were beautiful. The king had three wives. They were a pasha's daughter, a commoner, and the princess of Canossa, a Neapolitan-born opera singer who claimed to have married the king in 1957. He divorced the first two that he married. He was known to have numerous affairs.

The king had one hundred cars, military jeeps, thousands of acres of land, and a dozen of palaces. He was king of Egypt from 28 April 1936 to 26 July 1952. He became king at age sixteen. He died in exile in Rome, Italy, in March 1965.

After Farouk's abdication, the monarchy had been de facto abolished. In 1953, it was formally abolished, and a republic was declared. The new regime quickly auction off the king's vast collection of trinkets and stolen treasures. Among the most famous of those possessions was one of the United States's rare 1933 double eagle coin. The coin disappeared before it could be returned to the United States.

Toward the end of World War II, while Harry was assigned in Cairo, Egypt, he flew military personnel several times for a few days of R & R in Israel and went back to get them. He'd stay overnight in this one particular home. He got well acquainted with the family and their two children. The lady only had one bar of bathing soap. Harry wanted to get them something for staying with them. Knowing the lady needed bathing soap, which she was unable to get, when he got back to the commissary, he purchased a case of bathing soap and, on the next trip, took it to them. Harry said the lady teared up and offered to pay for the soap.

Unbeknownst to anyone, the Great War ended with the use of the atomic bomb. Cairo, Egypt, Harry said, they were held there until after the second bomb was dropped. The first uranium gun-type atomic bomb was dropped on Hiroshima 6 August 1945, followed by a plutonium implosion-type bomb on the city of Nagasaki on 9 August. No one knew about the atomic bombs other than a very few. President Truman had no knowledge of them until he became president.

The bombing of Japan accelerated the decision to surrender and saved many cadets' lives although some historians have argued that peace could have been made without dropping the bombs. Many veterans say it saved not only thousands of American lives but also thousands, probably millions, of Japanese lives. The Japanese had a code in which they felt it was an honor to die for the emperor. They just soon fight to the death or commit suicide rather than surrender. It leaves reasons why the atomic bomb was certainly justified when President Truman decided on dropping them. The memories and visions of what happened to innocent people, men, women, and little children, who were starved and killed because of unbridled hatred. The deployment of the atomic bombs would end the hostilities. They are unforgettable memories of those that experienced the war as the arduous sixty-five-mile Bataan Death March to prison camps on 9 April 1942.

Harry's sister-in-law, Neva Lilly Fritsche, went to Washington, DC, right after college and got a job as a private secretary of a man that was head of the Office Scientific Research Development. Unbeknownst to Neva, they were developing the atomic bomb; that no one knew of about until after the bombs were dropped—the secret world of scientists. Scientist gathered together and worked to produce the atomic bomb in great secrecy. Carlyn Canham's sister is ninety-five and lives in Ohio.

One of Harry's first assignments—with three others—was to fly airplanes for American people stationed at Karachi, India. They flew through South America to Karachi, India, known as the City of Lights; it is famously known as the city that never sleeps. The city is a higher hub of education in South Asia and the Muslin world. The second largest city in the world within city limits. They flew out to Ascension Island, a small island. Harry recalls the island as being five miles wide and three miles long.

Harry was at Ascension Island a lot. It was the way he'd fly to get across the South Pacific. He'd go down to Brazil go out to Ascension Island and on out to Africa. It depended on Africa where he was going. If he was going straight through to India, he'd go through Central Africa. If he was going to England, he'd fly on through North Africa.

The history of Ascension is influenced by military and strategic interest. The United States, in conformity with the United Kingdom, built a military airdrome: the Wideawake Field. It was during World War II. There were more than 25,000 aircraft of the United States Air Force that were transited through Ascension for transatlantic flights, with up to 4,000 armed forces, chiefly of American origins, posted on the island. In 1956, the United States came back with an agreement, allowing the Americans to enable the function of control devices while following up the path by missiles. Then in 1964, the Americans extended the landing strip to allow the landing of larger aircraft and that of the space shuttle. Also the strip was used for an emergency but never used by the shuttle.

Rain falls all year round; there are sudden gusts of wind that blow over the small island. Harry and his copilot went out there once and were going sixty through wind. And they weren't doing too well with the wind. Harry got on the runway and checked the engines and shut them down and topped off and was running out of gas taxiing. They always say "Go around" because of the downdraft in front. They tried to get Harry to go around, but he wouldn't go around because he knew he was out of fuel. Harry landed, and the base commander came running out to find out why Harry didn't do what he told him. He said, "What are you stopping out here for?" Harry responded, "I am out of gas."

For quite a ways, you can see the white stream cap around Ascension Island; the reason is that the wind generally is blowing. You can't see the island, just the white screen displayed by the wind around the island.

Harry and three others spent quite a night at Agra, India. Agra is the city of the Taj Mahal, in North Indian, a state of Uttar Pradesh, India. Agra is located on the banks of the Yamuna River. It is the hottest towns in India. It was monsoon weather. While asleep in a tent, water came up to their cot. The four were in their shorts with no clothing. They lost their ID, money, and clothing. It was at night. The four walked a mile to the base office in their shorts. They got along pretty good. The fellow at the base said, "I know someone that runs a place where we can get some clothes. I'll run over there and get them."

The fellow from the base office brought back some flying clothes, and they felt they were pretty well dressed. The next morning, he got them some shoes. They did pretty well, but when you lose your clothes, ID, licenses, and money, it takes a long time to get them back. They could write out a ticket for the airlines, for they had high priority, but you don't want to get on an airline without much on. They finally got clothes to come home, new ID, drivers' licenses, and money. Harry said to try to tell someone of what happened, and they'd think it is funny.

During World War II, Harry flew B-26s or some kind of combat aircraft. He flew all-night missions that were classified top secret. As the war came to an end in Europe, along with others, Harry elected to return to reserve status, which was very short-lived. Harry said, "I flew more hours in the active reserves than my friends in the active air force from 1946 until I was recalled to active duty in 1951."

Harry's brother, Morris, returned home in July 1945. He served with the 555th Bomb Squadron, 386 Bomb Group, as a tail gunner in Martin B-26 Marauder (medium bomber) and Douglas A-26 Invader (light bomber) and as an aerial gunnery instructor 2554. The 386 Bomb Group included 552nd, 553rd, 554th, and 555th. On 2 October, the 386th Bomb Group moved to Beaumont-sur-Oise (A-60) Airfield, France. Col. Thomas G. Corbin was commander of the 386th Bombardment Group from 25 August 1944 to 1945. With the 386th moved to the Continent on October 1944, the group attacked strong points, assaulted such objectives as defended areas, storage depots, and communications with primary focus on bridges during the Battle of the Bulge. For each of the campaigns in Northern France, the Ardennes, Rhineland, and Central Europe, he was awarded a Bronze Star.

After the war, Morris returned home, finished school, and became a professional engineer. While at school, he met Helen Murray and got married. They had three daughters, Elizabeth, Pam, Linda, and one son, James, "Jim." Elizabeth is a nurse in Illinois. Pam is in real estate on Cape Cod, Massachusetts, and Linda lives in Florida. Jim, as his father, is an engineer. Jim is senior vice president with Alder Benesch & Company in East Lancing, Michigan. Jim lives in Chicago, Illinois. He has a degree in ocean engineering. He studied the design of ships and deep-sea vehicles until in his senior year, he switched to onshore structures. His career has always been in civil engineering, mostly in roads and bridges. During his twenty-three years with the Illinois Tollway, he was also involved with buildings and mechanical electrical, but for most part, roads and bridges. Jim plays a major role in shaping our nation's infrastructure and local communities.

Son Jim said, "My father did not like to talk about the war, so I knew very little growing up. After he passed away, my mom gave me his things to look through, and I got very interested in what he did in WWII. I took the list of combat missions and was able to get some information from a historian. His name is Chester P. Plier. I knew very little growing up. I have to say, I am very proud of my father and my uncle for their service to our great nation and providing me a safe place to raise my family. I love them very much. I am also very proud of my father for the man he was, very professional, gave a lot back to his community and many organizations, was a fantastic dad, and I miss him a lot."

Morris kept a record of dates, time of some target missions, pilot's name, and number of the aircraft that he flew in his own handwriting. Morris listed fourteen missions, thirteen to Germany and one to Stod, Czechoslovakia. Morris knew the dangerous group formations headed for targets over Germany, air group sandwiching between layers of clouds and flak corridors.

Harry's graduation picture from flying school on 5 December 1943.

Harry in uniform, 1943.

BT 13 trainers, 1944.

Albert and Opal Canham, son Harry, and daughter, Ruth.

Harry standing alongside his DeSoto car, 1944.

Morris H. "Jim" Canham, 1943.

L-R: Harry, Opal, and Morris H. "Jim" Canham, 1943.

L-R: Charles Comerford, Harry Canham, George Demsey, Italo Bragalone, and Dante Bulli.

L-R: Harry Canham, George Demsey, Marilyn Bragalone, Dante Bulli, and Charles Comerford. Taken by Italo Bragalone.

10. *L-R:* Harry's son, Marc Canham, Opal (Harry's mother), and Harry, 1964.

Chapter Four

Recall to Active Duty

When the war ended in Europe and the Pacific, you'd thought that would surely end all war conflicts and that centralized control by a dictatorial authority had been dealt such a defeat that never again would a tyrant seek to gain power to start another war. But sadly that was not to be. To fight aggression is not easy but costly.

On 8 December 1945, Harry was commissioned an officer and applied for USAA insurance. At that time, it was only issued to officers. Military people were considered high risk until 11 August 2008 when all military people and their families became eligible for USAA insurance.

In 1951, Harry was recalled to active duty and sent to Upper Heyford air force base, located five miles northwest of Bicester, near the village of Oxfordshire, England, at a Royal Air Force station. It was a base for the United States Air Force Strategic throughout the 1950s, where Harry served as base operations officer. While stationed on temporary duty in England, he would fly the C-130 to the Russian border. Harry says the Russians flew a similar aircraft, and the pilots would try to be friendly. Flying back and forth took up all our time. It was during the Korean War.

Harry flew, making general air squad drops of personnel. He had expected to spend a six-month tour in England; instead it turned into two years. After the European war, Harry was sent to Korea with his squadron for three weeks. In Korea, a three-star general wanted Harry to drop him in the water. The general was the first person to drop on IP (initial point) area and went clear out of sight in the water. One of the crewmen said, "Oh, boss, you dropped him in the water!"

That night, the general saw Harry and came over where he was and told Harry thanks that he dropped him right where he wanted to be dropped. Harry says the general never thought that Harry would actually drop him.

During the time Harry was stationed in England, the airmen had a place where they would go to congregate. The general asked Harry, "Do you know anything about this place? Have you been down there?" Harry told him, "I know about it, but I haven't been down there, but I will go." The general said, "I think that would be a good idea to go down there and see."

Harry went down there and took a big black guy for protection. He said, it was an unusual place, but he didn't see anything wrong. The guys were having a good time. And Harry said, "They wanted to give me one, two, or three girls."

Harry went back and told the general what he saw going on, but he never went back. The general thought maybe they were up to no good, for there were times the men got to drinking too much and started scuffling. The military tried to keep a check on these types of places to make sure the fellows were not fighting or stuff. If they did, the place was shut right down.

In December 1953, Harry was reassigned to return to the United States, stationed at Barksdale air base in Bossier City, Louisiana, with the Third SSS (Strategic Support Squadron) flying C-124s, the largest aircraft in the United States Air Force or anywhere at that time. He was an air force commander, flight instructor, and operations officer of the Strategic Air Squadron.

The C-124 Globemaster II was a heavy-lift military transport aircraft built by Douglas Aircraft Company in Long Beach, California. The airlift was a critical tool. It was the United States Air Force Military Transport Service. From 1950 to the early 1960s, the C-124 was used extensively during the Vietnam War, transporting material from the United States to Vietnam. They were the only aircraft that could transport very large loads until C-5A became operational. The aircraft design featured two large clamshell doors and a hydraulically actuated ramp in the nose as well as a cargo elevator under the aft fuselage; the seventy-seven-feet cargo bay featured two overhead hoists, each capable of lifting eight thousand pounds. The aircraft could handle bulky and outside cargo, vehicles, bulldozers, trucks, field guns, tanks, and up to 123 litter patients plus 45 ambulatory patients, and 15 medical attendants or 200 fully equipped troops. Harry says the C-124 aircraft was capable of carrying 495 people.

The C-124's five-member crew named it Old Shaky because of the constant in-flight shaking, rattling, and squeaking. With the combat radius of a thousand miles, this allowed cargo or troops to a remote base and return without refueling. The C-124s provided heavy airlift during the Korean War and the Southeast Asia War, plus several other as refugee evacuation, mercy flights, and elsewhere throughout the world following any natural disaster. Old Shaky would serve protecting her country well.

Harry was promoted to major in 1953. The primary mission of the Third Strategic Support Squadron was the movement of nuclear weapons that was a very interesting and challenging duty for Harry. Gen. Curtis LeMay was the commander in charge of Strategic Air Command.

With World War II declared, Lt. Col. LeMay trained the 305th Bombardment Group and led them in 1942 as they deployed to England as part of the Eighth Air Force. Lemay aided in developing the key defenses formations, such as the combat box, used by the B17s during missions over Europe. In 1943, he was promoted to brigadier general. Known for his bravery in combat, LeMay personally led several missions as the Schweinfurt-Regensburg raid before he transferred to the China-Burma-India theater in 1944 to command the new XX Bomber Command based in China, where he oversaw B-29 raids on Japan's home islands.

With the capture of the Marianas Islands, LeMay was transferred to the XXI Bomber Command in January 1945. LeMay's B-29s routinely struck targets in Japanese cities operating from bases on Guam, Tinian, and Saipan. LeMay's tactics were endorsed by Presidents Roosevelt and Truman as a method for destroying war industry and preventing the need to invade Japan.

Postwar, General LeMay served administrative positions before being assigned to command the United States Air Forces in Europe. He organized air operations for the Berlin airlift after the Soviets blocked all ground access to the city. Once the airlift was up and running, LeMay was assigned to head up the Strategic Air Command (SAC), and he established his headquarters at Offutt Air Force Base, Nebraska. LeMay found the Strategic Air Command in poor condition and set about transforming SAC into the United States Air Force's premier offensive weapon. For the next nine years, LeMay oversaw the acquisition of a fleet of all-jet bombers and creation of a new command and control system that allowed for an unprecedented level of readiness. As the United States's principal means of delivering nuclear weapons, SAC built numerous new airfields and developed ballistic missile to Strategic Air Command inventory and incorporating them as a vital element of the nation's nuclear arsenal.

While assigned at Barksdale Air Force Base in Bossier City, Louisiana, Harry was sent to Albuquerque, New Mexico, with a load of weapons. They had just gotten unloaded and crew was without crew rest. The commander, General LeMay, called on the hardstand lot, where they were working out, saying, "I need you to do something. I need you to go to Loring Air Force Base and pick up some weapons out there—they are leaking." Harry said, "Sure." General LeMay said, "I've got food coming, and you can have something to eat on the way up, and I'll have food for you up there."

From Albuquerque, New Mexico, Harry flew clear across the United States over to Canada and flew in a traffic pattern to Loring Air Force

Base. That is how far up it was. The base was a United States Air Force installation in northeastern Maine, near Limestone and Caswell, Maine, in the United States. It was one of the largest bases of the United States Air Force's Strategic Air Command during its existence with many amenities. The base was home to a civilian population, who were employed alongside active service members. The traffic pattern is used for air safety that pilots follow when taking off or landing while maintaining visual contact with the airfield.

When Harry and his crew got up to Maine, Loring Air Force Base, the weather was terrible—below minimum. They thought they would send them somewhere else to land but instead was cleared to land. When they went to land on the runway, it was solid ice. All Harry had control of was reverse. They finally got to the other end of the runway, and they wanted Harry to shut down the engines, but he couldn't because the wind was blowing so bad it kept cocking the nose of the plane. There were factors beyond a pilot's control: wind, speed, and cloud cover. Harry had to get a tractor hooked on to the nose so he could shut down and go ahead and load the weapons. Harry said, "Finally, we got them to understand. You know, it is hard sometimes to converse with them on the ground."

It was sleeting and snowing, and they got turned around and headed down the runway; it was still all right. They tried to figure out where they could go and stop if they lost an engine or something. This time they couldn't do that; if they got started, there was no stopping, and so they just kept going. Harry told the crew, "When we hit sixty—*we're going for it!*" They got off all right without losing an engine, and about ten hours later, they got in with three weapons instead of one with five doctors onboard. They were trying to keep the crew separated from the weapons. They were dangerous. They kept the air going over the weapons, and Harry and his crew had everything opened in front so it would blow out the back. Harry says, "Honestly, it didn't get all blown out the back of the plane. I lost all my crew *long* before I got out of service."

Harry, being the lone survivor of his crew, went to the air force when he got bladder cancer and tried to tell the doctors in the air force.

They told Harry, "We agree with you. You are probably 100 percent right, but prove it." Every time Harry would go to prove it—they would disapprove it. The VA took care of Harry and got him in the right place for help. Harry has had seven bladder surgeries to remove cancer. His seventh surgery was in 2012. He went for a checkup every six months. Harry said, "I have been fortunate . . . I am still alive."

Harry had to get clearance from all over to carry or pick up weapons; it was so top secret. It was very dangerous because of the weapons leaking. While assigned with the Third Strategic Support Squadron, he carried weapons for six years. Harry never knew when he may be called out on a mission after a quick briefing. He was on call 24-7. Harry's flight mission through Canada was the only day flight that he ever made. He flew all night missions.

As for the weather, it could be a problem at times. Missions could be stymied by mud, snow, freezing rain, fog, wind, and intense heat. Many times, weather and fog grounded missions, especially day missions. The United States had radio operators stationed in Greenland predicting weather from their studies in the Arctic that helped. The contrails didn't bother Harry flying night missions as those aircrews that flew the daytime missions. Harry said early on fog used to block the vision out a lot. They just couldn't shoot for the clouds underneath them. It was dangerous because a shell coming out of the fog couldn't be seen. You can't duck it, and you couldn't do any good until they got the television sensor, FLIR (forward-looking infrared), and radar that allowed the gunship to visually electronically identify ground forces and targets in adverse weather and at night. Harry said, "It worked great! I took it out the first night that they got it on the airplane and got it working."

Brig. Gen. William H. Best, Jr., commander of the global Air Weather Service managed a worldwide network of weather. He graduated from Princeton University in 1941 with a bachelor of arts degree in mathematics. He enlisted in the US Army Air Corps in August 1942. In September 1943, he graduated from aviation cadet course in meteorology at the Massachusetts Institute of Technology and was commissioned a second lieutenant. He also managed the environmental faculties to support the United States Air Force and Army units. In addition to traditional weather support, Air Weather Service observes and forecasts space environment events, performed aerial reconnaissance of hurricanes and typhoons, and carried out atmosphere sampling. His prime function was to assist and advise decision makers whose decisions are affected by the aerospace and natural environment.

From 1943 to 1946, General Best served as weather officer in the Pentagon Weather Central. He was relieved from active military service in 1946 and worked as a United States Weather Bureau meteorologist and was weather staff officer for the Colorado Air National Guard in Denver, Colorado.

In 1947, General Best was recalled to active duty in 1947 through 1949; he was chief forecaster at the US Air Force Weather Central in Haneda, Tokyo, Japan. After graduation from the air tactical school in Tyndall Air Force Base, Florida, in 1950, he became assistant operations officer for the 210d Weather Group at Mitchel air base, New York. General Best then entered New York University under the Air Force Institute of Technology program, and he received his master of science degree in meteorology and was assigned to the Air Weather Service headquarters in Washington, DC, in July 1951.

Brig. Gen. Best's center of focus was solidly on the science of meteorology. He entered the University at Stockholm, Sweden, in 1954 under the Air Force Institute of Technology doctorate-level program. He was one of the first United States Air Force officers to be selected. General Best was assigned to the 2d Weather Wing in Germany in 1955 and became assistant technical services officer. In October 1957, he returned to the United States and assumed command of the Detachment 30, 5th Weather Group at Westover Air Force Base, Massachusetts. In 1960, General Best entered the Air War College at Maxwell Air Force Base, Alabama, and in 1961, became duty commander of the Fourth Weather Group at Andrews Air Force Base, Maryland. He returned to Westover Air Force Base in 1963 and was assigned as commander of the Eighth Weather Squadron and staff weather officer for the Strategic Air Commander's Eighth Air Force.

From Westover, he was assigned to Scott Air Force Base, Illinois, in 1966, where he served as commander of the Weather Wing. In 1967, he was assigned to Headquarters Air Weather Service as deputy chief of staff for operations, and in 1970, he became vice commander of the global weather service.

His decorations and awards included the Legion of Merit and Air Force Commendation Medal. In 1971, he was awarded the Vietnamese Air Force Distinguished Service Order, First Class, for the United States Air Force Air Weather Service's achievement in organizing and training a Vietnamese Air Force meteorological service.

General Best was promoted to brigadier general in 1970, retired 1 August 1973, and died at age seventy-five on 21 January 1995. He was a member of Sigma Xi, the honorary scientific fraternity, and an honor student of the US Air Force Air War College. He was past councilor (1968–1971) and former executive committeeman of the American Meteorological Society as well as a member of the Society's Planning Commission and an elected American Meteorological Society (AMS) fellow, the highest level of professional membership. General Best's meteorology achievements did a lot for all branches of the United States military in helping to accomplish successful missions.

After being briefed, during the night, aerial scouts were sent to fly a weather reconnaissance mission and gather information for a scheduled combat mission. They were dangerous missions. A single aircraft's mission was to fly without any fighter escort. They would fly to the enemy lines and record temperatures, cloud cover, winds aloft at various altitudes, and icing conditions that they'd transmitted to headquarters in code at regular intervals—on through a whole weather checklist. Missions require careful monitoring to help decide what to hit and when. Aerial reconnaissance often provide a more accurate assessment of weather conditions than radar or satellite imaging, which are only short-term—up to four hours.

Chapter Five

Air Corps Independence

During World War II, the United States Organization (USO) provided live entertainment to the United States troops and provided local bands and movies during peacetime. The USO club was a place to go dance, attend social events, watch movies, and listen to music. It was designed to remind the military men of home (GIs' home away from home). It was founded by President Roosevelt to provide morale for our military men. USO was sometimes located in combat zones. During World War II, Korean War, and the Vietnam War, the military was provided entertainment. Singers and Hollywood stars volunteered to perform for the troops and their families; that continues today. It was a diversion to help relieve the stresses of war. Although this was provided, many men in the military did not see these shows.

The air arm of the United States Army known as the United States Army Air Corps (USAA) became the Army Air Forces (AAF) in June 1941, where all personnel and units were under a single commanding general, an airman, Henry H. Arnold, from 1941 to 1946, and Carl Spaatz, from 1946 to 1947. The air force didn't become a separated branch of the military until after the war when General George Marshall decided to revamp the military and summoned Gen. Alexander "Sandy" Patch to Washington, DC.

General Marshal appointed General Patch to a postwar board called the Patch Board to reshape the military. It was the beginning of *independence* for the air corps. The land forces generals and the navy were vehemently opposed to the separation in 1941. The navy would remain opposed of the independence. The air force liked the separation.

General Patch never lived to see his recommendations go into effect on President Truman's order September 18, 1947, when the United States Air Force became a separate and equal element of the United States Armed Forces. Patch died of exhaustion and pneumonia, and surely a broken heart, on November 21, 1945, at age fifty-five. His only son, also a West Point graduate, took part in the Normandy battle. Capt. Alexander M. "Mac" Patch II, with the 315th Infantry Regiment, Seventy-Ninth Infantry Division, was wounded twice and earned a Purple Heart with two Oak Leaf Clusters. Captain Patch was under General Patton's command when he was injured the first time. His father read about it in the *Stars and Stripes* newspaper. General Patch brought his son from England to recuperate near him. While Mac was recuperating, the Seventy-Ninth Infantry was reassigned to his father's command. In October 1944, Captain Patch was killed within a few days of his return to action. He was buried in Epinal American Cemetery, Epinal, France.

When Gen. George C. Marshall called General Patch to Washington, his heart was to return to the Pacific where he had demonstrated a great deal of drive on Guadalcanal. Patch achieved the distinction of winning the first American land victory of WWII on Guadalcanal in early 1943. In March 1943, Patch was designated the commander of the Seventh Army for the invasion of Southern France. General Patch's Seventh Army advanced nearly four hundred miles up the Rhône River Valley in less than a month, landing on the southern coast, and moved up the eastern side of France and linked with General Patton's Third Army in on Northern France in a tank battle on a rolling countryside, creating a solid wall of Allied forces, stretching from Antwerp to the Swiss border in September 1944.

General Patch commanded the Seventh Army in the area south of the Battle of the Bulge and through the Vosges Mountains, low Vosges, to V-day. It was the first time in history for any troops to go over the

Vosges Mountains. Patch's troops had been near there in World War I. General Patch did his job quietly and worked laboriously, not trying to attract the spotlight. In history, his great record remains as he lived, quietly and without fanfare.

Patch threw himself into directing the board, traveling to interview prominent civilians, officers, and generals all over. Generals George C. Marshall, Mark Clark, Eisenhower, Patton, MacArthur, Devers, and others as secretary of war, Robert P. Patterson. Patch was known to throw himself into a job and never wavered through an assignment. One of General Patch's recommendations was the air force to be made separate from the army.

Sadly, there are many stories that have gone unrecognized in history. General Patch's name never stood in the line with the famous people when it should have from his splendid career record. World War II ended on General Patch's Seven Army segment at Dachau concentration camp and where the battle for Munich ended on 1 May 1945 in Europe. From the horrible Dachau death camp and the heaps of ruin at Munich, cradle of the Nazi feast, General Patch moved his Seventh Army onto Salzburg, Austria. General Kesselring surrendered his troops to the Forty-fifth Infantry Division with support. On 7 May 1945, German top army officers went to General Eisenhower's headquarters in Reims, France, and signed unconditional surrender. World War II was a truly global conflict, a war that involved every aspect of human life. The famous Third (of which Audie Murphy, most decorated WWII soldier, is part) and Forty-fifth Infantry (Thunderbirds troops) served under General Patch's command in Germany.

For Harry to have the air force separated from the army was most welcome. He liked it much better with the air force being a separate branch of the military. President Harry Truman's signing the National Defense Act of 1947 and enabling legislation created a separate air force. There were new uniforms and new rank insignia. The air force was no longer under a ground commander with no flying experience. W. Stuart Symington was appointed the first secretary of the air force, independent of the War Department/Army.

James Vincent Forrestal was the last cabinet-level United States secretary of the navy and the first United States secretary of defense.

Upon arrival in England, many of our Army Air Corps men were greeted from Germany by radio broadcast with such propaganda as "What goes up must come down." Our United States Army Air Forces answered them on 8 May 1945; the war in Europe was over with Germany's unconditional surrender, unlike World War I that actually ended with more of a ceasefire or armistice than an actual surrender. The German Air Force was still undefeated and was actually superior to Allied air forces.

During World War II, voluntary crews of United States Air Forces fighters and bombers were dangerously doing their jobs—just as those involuntarily fighting in the Pacific jungles or foot in Europe. Unbelievably, the Army Air Forces's morale was high during World War II because of young, pragmatic leadership and the universal glamor accorded being an aviator. Young Canham chose to fly the skies of top secret missions in the face of constant danger. Today, those many, many missions are hard for Harry to single out and tell. Yet one can tell that Harry Canham has nothing but respect for his time served with the military. Harry took duty as a moral obligation. It was obvious that he had an asset of being able to mix judgment with rules and regulations, and duty was getting the job done.

Col. Harry Canham, in many ways, was of the similar mold as Gen. Alexander Patch. Harry cared and respected deeply those that he commanded. Harry took advantage of an academic and personal service that was provided in the Army Air Corps. Harry worked hard to practice good academic habits and stayed focused on events that were meaningful and encouraging in striving for his goal to fly. He did his job that he volunteered for and never flinched from an assignment. It was all about victory.

Harry knew the importance of a strong air force in using elements such as global reach, global vigilance, or global power. When combined, these elements heralded a turning point in the character of our nation's welfare. No other service can deliver the capability and capacity that our United States Air Force provides.

Since the World War II campaign, our air force projects global military power on a scale that our adversaries cannot match. Our air arms are supremely capable at what they do. With rapid global mobility, moving cargo and equipment, saving lives with highly skilled aeromedical transport teams has set a new standard for the survival of our wounded soldiers.

Our military today carry out all core mission areas through air, space, and cyberspace. Airmen in every flight play a critical role in providing airpower that is critically important with a decade's long asymmetric advantage with in every squadron, every wing, or in every major command.

The air force has served America's long-term security interests by giving our nation options to confront the challenges of a unpredictable future. It provides armed overwatch, close air support, mobility operations, and intelligence, surveillance and reconnaissance (ISR).

With constant attacks with new and capable threats emerging daily in the area of cyberweapons, antisatellite system, and electromagnetic jamming, our country's investments in air force capacities and readiness are essential if the nation is to maintain an agile, flexible, ready force. Air force airpower has readily been used to deter conflict and control escalation. Since the air force became independent from the Army Air Corps, it has been smaller, a smaller highly effective air force is clearly preferable to a larger one of lesser quality. Keeping our military well-funded is to protect the air operating in, from, and through the global domains of air, space, and cyberspace that are all geared to support our nation's security interest.

Chapter Six

Vietnam Mission: A Personal Tragedy

Major Canham was transferred to Second Air Force Headquarters at Barksdale Air Force Base in 1958. The air base was named in honor of World War I aviator and test pilot Lt. Eugene Hoy Barksdale. Barksdale died while flight-testing Douglas O-2 observation airplane over McCook Field in Dayton, Ohio. He had attempted a bailout from a fast spin only to get his parachute caught in and severed by the brace wire attached to the wings of the wing and fall to the ground.

At Barksdale Air Force Base, the F-4 fighter jet made its first flight on May 6, 1958. It is the largest airport in the world located on 23,000 acres east southeast of Bossier City, Louisiana. The famous Seventeenth Bomb Group trained at Barksdale Field, which would be led by Gen. Jimmy Doolittle during his raid on Tokyo. Harry's new duties at Barksdale Field consisted of two squadrons of C-124s and movements of atomic weapons. Harry was responsible for flying hours of all aircraft in the Second Air Force and allocation of aircraft for air shows.

Harry checked out in Lockheed F-80 Shooting Star Fighter, a single-seat fighter. The first turbojet-powered aircraft, a low-wing cantilever monoplane with a knife-edge laminar-flow wing section; engine within the rear fuselage; air intakes on each side of the fuselage of the wing leading edge, and retractable tricycle-type landing gear. USAAF/USAF first operational jet-powered aircraft set a world speed record in 1947. Lockheed T-33 Shooting Star (or T-Bird) a two-seater advanced American jet trainer aircraft was used for such tasks as drone director and target towing. Harry remained current in the C-124.

At Barksdale air base, Harry had lived off base for eight months. In 1961, he was sent with his family to Norfolk, Virginia, to attend Armed Forces Staff College, a great school with emphasis on the North Atlantic Treaty Organization (NATO). The North Atlantic Treaty Organization was an intergovernmental military alliance based on the North Atlantic Treaty. After graduation, Harry received orders for assignment to Naples, Italy, Air-South of NATO Command. The initial command post for AFSOUTH that consisted of land, sea, and air headquarters were all established in Italy.

NATO is a security alliance of twenty-eight countries from North America and Europe signed in 1949. A real threat for the Western countermeasures was the threat of aggression by the Soviet Union during the Cold War. The threat convinced American leaders to strengthen United States military forces, especially air power. The United States Air Force, in breaking the Soviet blockade of Berlin, demonstrated the value of air capabilities during the Cold War. NATO's goal was for a partnership is peace of the different countries and cooperation between Western Europe and Northern American nations for the good of freedom. Should an attack occur, each of the countries would come to the aid of the country being attacked.

Allied Forces Southern Europe (AFSouth) originally formed in 1951. From 1951 to 2003, the commander in chief of Allied Forces Southern Europe was always a United States navy admiral based in Naples. He also held the national appointment of commander in chief of the United States Naval Forces Europe. Allied Forces Southern Europe (AFSOUTH) was all established in Italy. Greece and Turkey joined the alliance in early part of 1952. Allied Land Forces South-Eastern Europe was created with its new land command headquarters based in Izmir, Turkey.

In 1952, the first AFSOUTH exercises took place with a series of military maneuvers involving operations of small ground unit tactical training, land-based tactical air support, and carrier-based air support under the overall command of Admiral Carney. Operations involved warships and aircraft and featured a large-scale amphibious assault along the western coast of Turkey. AFSOUTH continued to conduct exercises in the 1960s and 1970s, a five-nation naval and air exercise conducted throughout the Mediterranean in 1974. The United States contribution to the exercise was based on the USS *America* carrier battle group. From 1967, the overall shape of AFSOUTH did not significantly change until the command was renamed in the early part of the twentieth century. Due to political considerations, command of the naval forces in the region was split. Allied Naval Forces Southern Europe, at Naples, operated most of the NATO Allies's naval forces in the Mediterranean under an Italian admiral. Due to the United States's desire to retain control of their nuclear-armed naval forces, the United States Sixth Fleet reported directly to CINCAFSOUTH, supported by a separate headquarters named Naval Striking and Support Forces Southern Europe (STRIKFORSOUTH).

As of 2013, the commanders of the Allied Joint Force Command Naples is responsible for conducting the full range of military operations throughout NATO area of responsibility and beyond in order to prevent aggression and to contribute to the effective defense of NATO territory and forces, safeguard freedom of the seas and economy lifelines, and to maintain or restore the security of NATO nations.

During Harry's assignment in Naples, there were service people and their families from each branch of the United States Armed Forces. The air force personnel were assigned to elements of the Air Force South. Harry's family was with him while living on base. With knowing the cultural differences, the general asked Harry's wife, Betty, a schoolteacher, to take the women shopping. He knew with her Latin knowledge it would help the other women while in a non-English-speaking region with the speech barrier. Betty shopped with the women in Italy, Europe, and stateside, and enjoyed it.

Betty was a great supporter of Harry's job and had a great love for the air force. Son, Michael, said his dad would call his mother saying he would be bringing some military people home with him for dinner, and his mother would always say okay. They may have to have a drink before dinner was ready, but she always provided a nice meal.

Harry and Betty were both from the Wataga, Illinois, area but unaware of each other. They met at a dance while Betty was home from college. Harry danced with her and later said, "I am going hunting." Betty asked Harry with whom, and he told her. She said, "That is my father and brother."

It was at Betty's brother Shorty Woolsey's grocery that Harry and friends heard about in the Japanese attack on Pearl Harbor. It was a day that would change Harry's life and fulfill his dream to fly.

Harry's son Mike went to a Catholic boarding school (Notre Dame), and son Marc went to a local school in Naples during Harry's three-year assignment. The boys were well prepared for college. The schools were for all foreign children. There were civilian workers, military, and Saudi Arabia oil businesspeople's children all going to school at Naples. Saudi Arabia didn't have a school. Michael said in twelve years, he went to fourteen different schools.

While Harry was stationed in Naples, Italy, with the Southern Command of NATO, a four-star admiral was his superior. The admirals had a captain and chief in the front office that Harry shot skeet with. They were the ones that told the admiral about Harry. They said they were having trouble with running the rod and gun club, to which Harry said, "I don't need another job."

Harry was an international referee for skeet shooting. There were two skeet squads of five-man squad teams; some had two, and some had three skeet teams. The men were someone that was affiliated with the military along with the civilians and contractors. It cost money to put up a team as they had to practice so much. They had a skeet team to shoot in Germany and Italy. Harry did a lot of skeet shooting.

The military during World War II used skeet shooting to teach gunners the principles of leading and timing on a flying target. The training course would help soldiers to get more proficient in their shooting, and therefore, the skeet shooting clubs were formed for a competitive shooting sport. During Harry's gunnery course program, his firing accuracy was so exact that they wanted him to go into infantry instead of the air force. He told them, "I want to fly!"

The admiral had Harry to do things for him, and Harry would do them in quick order. The admiral was impressed with Harry's interest. The admiral called Harry in, and while they were talking, the admiral mentioned about carrier landing. Harry said, "I have watched them practice on takeoff and return. I have never done that, but I would like to." The admiral said, "Well, you are about to. I am going to send you out on a carrier." Harry said, "I have to ask my boss." The admiral said, "I have taken care of that."

Harry's boss was a two-star, and the admiral was a four-star, so he wasn't worried about that. The admiral sent Harry on an airplane out to the carrier and left him there to receive naval aircraft experience. When Harry arrived out there, he was told to come on out to the carrier. There was just one airplane but a bunch of little ships.

The instructor pilot was waiting for Harry for he had been briefed that Harry was coming. He had recognized the name and was a friend of Harry's. While in training school, they stayed on opposite ends of the barracks. Harry said, "He flew every mission off the navy carrier with me—thank God!"

Harry says, "Flying off the carrier is a different way of life. The first time we came back from being up north of the Mediterranean on a big exercise, Harry saw what looked like a flashlight down below and asked, "Is that the ship down there?" The answer was yes!

Harry asked, "Where you are going to land?" The instructor responded, "Where *you* are going to land!"

Navy pilots trained on a runway before going to the carrier. Harry trained performing landing and takeoffs on the carrier and *never* learned to relax. He flew all night flights. They practiced on the runway that had been marked off. You came in and got stopped before you got to that light, and if you didn't, you were in the water. Harry flew eight missions in the F-4 Fathom fighter in and off the carrier and said, "It is a tough life aboard the ship, a hair-rising experience. I had watched them practice and practice. But I never knew that I would be doing it."

In 1963, Harry returned to the United States with his family and was assigned to Langley Air Force Base, Virginia, with duty in the US Air Force Tactical Air Command (TAC) command post, which prepares and maintains combat-ready forces capable of conducting worldwide tactical air operations. A command post is where the commander of TAC, then Gen. Walter C. Sweeney, Jr., directs and controls the operations of a number of air forces and air bases under his command. Harry was kept very busy and said it was an interesting place to work.

While commander of his strategic bomber force, in June 1954, General Sweeney led a trio of Stratojets in history's first nonstop flight of jet bombers across the Pacific Ocean. After different assignments, it was at Langley Air Force Base, Virginia, in October 1961, when Sweeney was promoted to four-star general and assumed command of the Tactical Air Command with headquarters at Langley Air Force Base.

General Sweeny became ill with cancer and stayed at Langley base for six weeks. Harry was with him in his office going over some things, and Sweeney could hardly get out of the chair and said, "When you can't get out of your chair, it is time to quit."

General Sweeney was the one sponsor that put Harry in for a promotion. He retired 1 August 1965, and died 22 December 1965. The Boulevard at Langley base was changed in General Sweeny's memory: Langley Air Force Base, 37 Sweeney Boulevard.

It was at Langley Air Force Base that Harry was promoted to lieutenant colonel in 1966 and assigned chief of command post. In 1967, he was sent to C-130 school in Tennessee, a three-month school. Harry was reassigned to Virginia Langley Air Force Base, C-130 tactical wing, where he continued C-130 training. This was tactical operations—i.e., formation flying, dropping paratroopers (all services), short-field landing (assault landing), training for Vietnam on the conditions that were encountered in the war. Upon completion of combat training, he was sent to Southeast Asia.

On the first of August in 1967, Harry delivered a cargo shipment to Vietnam; the weather was terrible, lots of rain and mud everywhere. It was during the monsoon season. Harry had gotten out of the airplane and was helping unload the ammunition when he was injured. A forklift was being used to help unload the shipment when the driver of the forklift accidently ran over Harry's right shoulder, side, and leg. Harry was airlifted to a hospital in Vietnam, where a surgeon was going to amputate Harry's leg. Another doctor at the hospital thought that Harry's injury was too much for them and had him flown back stateside to the United States Air Force Hospital, Scott Air Force Base, in Illinois. He was there in the hospital from 1 August 1967 to 21 December 1967. He never lost his leg and said, "The mud is what saved me."

Upon Harry's release from the hospital in December 1967, he was sent to Pope Air Force Base, North Carolina, as squadron pilot with the C-130E aircraft, 779 TAC Airlift Squadron. In April 1968, he was assigned squadron operations officer, 779 Tactical A/L Squadron. And in 1969, he was made squadron commander of 777 Tactical A/L Squadron. Harry would return with another shot at doing what he loved most—to fly.

Chapter Seven

Ubon, Thailand Assignment

A general from the Pacific had Harry fly him to a southern base in California. During the flight, the general told Harry he was being assigned commander of an AC-130 gunship in Southeast Asia. Harry asked, "Who else was selected?" The general said, "You".

February of 1970, Harry was promoted to colonel and transferred to 4442 Combat Crew Training, Little Rock Air Force Base, Arkansas, as wing director of operations and wing deputy commander of operations, 314 TAC Airlift Wing, consolidated 4442 into 314 Tactical Airlift Wing. Harry taught at the Little Rock Air Force Base from February 1970 to December 1971. Everyone came in thinking they could get in that school, but they couldn't. It was an air force school. Harry said, "What the air force does if they have fifteen in the school, they'll give them four or five names they can put in, and we tell them who it'll be, and they'll put it in their books and send down to qualify."

While Colonel Canham was stationed at the Little Rock Air Force Base, an Israel Defense Force group of six men and their commander were at the base. Israel had purchased airplanes, and the training came with the purchase. Harry invited the group over for dinner before they left. When the food went around the first time, the men hardly ate any food. Harry noticed it and said something to the commander. He told Harry they are just checking to see if they liked it; they can't leave food on their plate. He said, "The next time that they come through, just give them a minute, they will clean you out," which they did!

The Israeli commander gave Harry a nice hard copy of their *Six-Day War*, saying, "This is *our* version of it, not *your* version." Harry said it was different.

Six weeks later, the commander was back over and went out to see Harry. They were talking about one of the crewmen, and the commander said, "Well, unfortunately we had lost him. He had been sent out on a mission and lost in combat."

In December 1971, Col. Harry Canham was assigned squadron commander of the Sixteenth Special Operations Squadron in Ubon, Thailand, AC-130 aircraft Gunships; was also wing (Eighth TAC Fighter Wing) department commander for bomber/gunships, B-57/C-130 aircraft; and wing department commander for Special Operations, Eighth TAC Fighter Wing.

Colonel Canham would return to Vietnam, flying the AC-130E gunship (known as the Cadillac). The Lockheed AC-130E gunship used in Vietnam was a heavily armed ground attack aircraft. Harry had shot it down at school when he took a student out to test the aircraft. When they got one over in Vietnam, Harry had already flown the gunship, so he flew it right away. It had different shells that they could shoot. It was the first model to have the 105-mm howitzer cannon. It was an artillery piece of the army as they said, "Shoot it over the hill." They had to adjust a few things because the guns pointed down a little, and so they put a stopper in there so it wouldn't go on out. It was an awesome gunship with its close observation eyes and effective firepower. It was large aircraft. Harry said, "Some pilots like to fly the ones that go fast. I like to fly the big ones. The bigger they come, the better I like them."

The C-130s basic airframe was manufactured by Lockheed while Boeing was responsible for the conversion into a gunship and for aircraft support. During the 1950s, the C-130 Hercules was originally designed as an assault transport power plant. It was readily adapted for uses in a variety of other roles. The turboprop was a new application of turbine engines that used exhaust gases to turn a propeller; it offered greater range at propeller-driven speeds compared to pure turbojets that were faster. The C-130 is a four-engine turboprop military aircraft designed and built by Lockheed, now Lockheed Martin. The aircraft entered service with the United States in the 1950s and was capable of using unprepared runways for takeoffs and landings and originally designed as troop, medical evacuation, and cargo transport aircraft. The versatile airframe has found uses in different roles, including as an AC-130 gunship.

Model C-130A was powered by Allison T56-A-9 turboprops with three-blade propellers and originally equipped with the blunt nose of the prototypes. As it became operational with Tactical Air Command (TAC), its lack of range became apparent and additional fuel capacity was added in the form of external Pylon-mounted tanks at the end of the wing. In December 1956, the C-130A was delivered until 1959's introduction of the C-130B model. It was developed to complete the A models. It incorporated new features, particularly increased fuel capacity in the form of auxiliary tanks built into the center wing section and an AC electrical system. Four-bladed standard propellers replaced the Aero Products three-bladed propellers that distinguished the earlier A models.

During the Vietnam War, C-130 Hercules replaced the Douglas AC-47 Spooky gunship (Project Gunship I) to improve mission endurance and increase capacity to carry ammunitions. It was capable of flying faster than helicopters and at high altitudes with excellent loiter time; the use of the pylon turn allowed the AC-47 to deliver continuous accurate fire to a single point on the ground.

In 1962, the extended-range C-130E model entered service as an interim long-range transport for the Military Air Transport Service. The B-model was reintroduced with the installation of 1,360 United States gallon Sargent Fletcher external fuel tanks under each wings' midsection and more powerful Allison T56-A-7A turboprops. The hydraulic boost pressure to the ailerons was reduced back to 2050 PSI as a consequence of the external tanks' weight in the middle of the wingspan. The E model also featured avionics upgrades and a higher gross weight.

In September 1967, under the Gunship II program, the first AC-130 gunship arrived in South Vietnam and began operations over Laos and Vietnam that year. Laos is a landlocked county in Southeast Asia, China to the northwest, Vietnam to the east, Cambodia to the south, and Thailand to the west.

The AC-130A (Project II) carried more technologically advanced sensor to allow it to more effectively engage the targets. The aircraft had a series conversions of modifications added: a direct night-vision telescope was installed in the forward door, an early forward-looking infrared (FLIR) in the forward part of the left wheel well, and with Gatling guns fixed facing down and aft along the left side.

The AC-130 gunship was first activated in Vietnam and later was advanced to the AC-130E and H models. The AC-130s primary missions were close air support, air interdiction and armed reconnaissance, and perimeter and point defense, escort landing, drop and extradition zone support, forward air control, limited command and control, and combat reach and recue. The E model also featured structural improvements, avionics upgrades, and a higher gross weight. In October 1968, enough gunships arrived to form a squadron called the Sixteenth Special Operations Squadron (SOS) of the Eighth Tactical Fighter Wing (TFW) at Ubon, Thailand. In 1969, both aircraft with the Project Black Spot and Black Crow began operations from 1969 till 1970; the Black Crow system staved into the targeting computers on the AC-130 A/E/H enabled the detection of trucks hidden under dense jungle foliage, typical along the Ho Chi Minh trail.

In 1970, AC-130As were acquired with the Pave Pronto Project. In the summer of 1971, Surprise-Package-equipped AC-130s were converted to the Pave Pronto configuration. When the gunship got overseas, some of the people wanted to try the gunship, and Harry told them, "No, you can't, the only place that you can do that is in air force school." They responded, "Well, the tech commander is coming over here, and we'll get on him." Harry said, "No, you can't do that!" They said, "Yes, we can!" The tech commander said the same thing. He told them, "Talk to this man [Harry], he ran that school. That is an air force school, not my school." They finally gave up. The navy, marines, and coast guard all get their training on the C-130 at the air force base in Arkansas, for it is the only C-130 school in the country.

The AC-130H gunships were heavily armed aircraft. Boeing modified the Spectre airframe with engine heat radiation shields, weapons for control center, weapons package, flare and chafe launch system, and specialized electronics including AUTV and a laser range finder, forward-looking infrared radar, located just below aft and extended left-front nose radome. These sensors allow the gunship to visually or electronically identify friendly ground forces and targets.

The Spectre deployed flares that were sometimes referred to as angles flares due to the distinctive flare shape. Gunships have been a part of some notable offensive. They are credited with many lifesaving close air-support missions in Vietnam and credited for destroying over ten thousand enemy trucks on the Ho Chi Minh trail.

The AC-130H aircraft was upgraded with new features by incorporating side-firing weapons from the left (port) side. It was integrated with sophisticated sensor, variegation, and fire control systems to provide surgical firepower or area saturation during extended periods at night and in adverse weather of the nonpressurized aircraft. During an attack, the gunship performs a pylon turn, flying in a large circle around the target, allowing it to fire at its target far longer than a conventional attack aircraft. The AC-130H Spectre was armed with two 20-mm cannons, one 40-mm autocannon, and one 105-mm artillery cannon.

The Ho Chi Minh trail was a logistic system that ran from North Vietnam to South Vietnam through the neighboring kingdom of Laos and Cambodia. The trail undeniably laid at the center of the war with the North Vietnamese transportation tons of supplies daily over the trail to the south. The trail existed for centuries as primitive footpaths located mostly in Laos. The United States could not block the trail with ground forces because the countries the trail passed through were officially neutral. The United States's extensive bombing did not prevent the trucks from moving with supplies during the night. The weather in southeastern Laos played a major role both in their supply effort and the United States and South Vietnamese efforts to confront and halt it.

The southwest monsoon brought heavy rains from mid-May to mid-September with overcast skies and high temperatures. The northwest monsoon, from mid-October to mid-March, was drier and lower temperatures that provided good movement of soldiers and supplies. The road within the trail was used to transport bulk of supplies even during the rainy season over asphalted or hard-packed roads allowing large supplies to be moved. There were numerous supply bunkers, hospitals, barracks, storage areas, command and control facilities all concealed from aerial observation. There was a nonstop replacement system of natural and man-made camouflage along the trail, allowing trucks to drive the entire length of the trail without emerging from the canopy except to cross streams or cross them on crude bridges built beneath the water's surface. A sparsely populated region of rugged mountain, triple canopy jungle, and dense primeval rain forest made it challenging.

While out flying around the Ho Chi Minh trail, Harry could see a convoy of thirty to thirty-five trucks on the radar coming down the mountainside. Harry told the fellows to get ready because he was going to get the first truck at the bottom and go around and get the top truck and corner the motorcade. Upon Harry's pushing the button, a gunner said, "You got them the first shot!" Harry got them stopped, and that was what he wanted; the drivers could be seen running. The fellows said, "There he goes—get him!" Harry replied, "I don't want those guys. I want all those trucks. It's what I want." The top truck had fuel, and it ran down, starting a fire that traveled down the whole line, and Harry didn't have to shoot another shot. Harry said, "I just backed off and watched—I had to get back away from it, for it kept coming closer. It was hotter than blue blazes—I just about shot myself down!"

Everything said on the airplane was recorded on tape. When the tape was played back, one of the United States senators who was there said, "The language needs to be cleaned up a little. When you go out tonight and jump in the airplane, you can tell them." Harry replied, "I am not going to say anything, and I don't think you better either!" The senator said, "We have women and senators up there." Harry replied, "Yah, I know that, if they can't listen to the tape, they'd better get out of the senate."

The gunship flown on mission was like one of those old C-130A models that you'd shoot like a gun, for it didn't have navigation sights on it and you have to move your gun around and shoot them—just like shooting a rabbit.

While assigned in Thailand, Harry had one of his aircrafts shot down, and a chopper crew went out to find them. They said it was just like Halloween with the men and parachutes up in the tree. The crew told them, "Stay on the tree, don't get down on the ground, we will get you down." They got beneath the tree, pulled a parachute out, got the fellow, put him in the chopper, and went to get another one. Here they were just picking the men right off the tree. The chopper crew were laughing about the parachutes landing on the tree, but they said it was the best thing that the parachutes came down there hiding the men.

One crewman was injured badly, and the plane had gotten really shot up. The pilot at the front told his crew to get out fast. Then he himself jumped. The pilot said when he jumped off, his parachute had just opened, and within twenty or thirty seconds, the airplane incinerated. The crew all survived. Harry said the pilot timed that just right. When catastrophe strikes a plane and puts the crew in danger, they must get out while the getting is good. If the pilot had waited another two minutes, they would have all died. As a pilot, Harry used his best to put forth safety for his crewmen, relying, as he did, upon them (faith) and staying focused to bring the aircraft home. Flak can be as personal as a bayonet when your plane is hit.

Harry would never know peace in Vietnam. While in Vietnam, Harry had guards on watch of several big manhole ground systems. One time, he went out in the jeep to check on his crew, and the guards stationed up high warned him that North Vietcong's were popping up out of the manholes. Harry always carried a gun with him. As they were popping up, he would pop them. He got six that night.

Guarding the airplanes in Vietnam was a big problem because the Vietcong would come up through those ground sewers, trying to put sticky bombs on the aircraft and blow them up. They had to keep vigilant coverage over the sewers for those little fellas were pretty shrewd.

Ships would run up and down the Mekong River until the gunship came out. They knew that it was out after them, and they would zap in the bushes right away. The ships would be loaded with ammunition and stuff. Harry could see the ships down there and shoot them. After a couple of ships had been hit, men would jump off the others and go ashore—anything to get away from the explosions. They didn't know they could be seen from the gunship's navigational device sensors that visually identifies targets and disguised between allied forces and enemy from a great distance any place at any time. Harry said, "My aim was to get rid of all the ammunition and tank equipment they were bringing down the river that was doing all the damage. The boats would catch fire, and the ammunition would start blowing up, and I'd get out of there. I got five boats—which was a good night for fishing."

Mekong River Valley region is one of the cradles of human civilization. The Mekong River is the lifeblood of Southeast Asia. It flows through six district geographical regions: China, Burma, Thailand, Laos, Cambodia, and Vietnam. During the Vietnam War, the west bank of the Mekong provided a basis for raids against the advance of the communist armies in Laos. The Mekong is one of the most biologically diverse areas in the world—second only to the Amazon River. The length of the river is 3,050 miles. Harry said he flew over it all the time.

All during Harry's time in Vietnam, he had a large pocketknife that he carried around his neck for two different reasons. First thing, if he went down, he'd have something to help get food with. Second thing, if he had to parachute out of the aircraft and the parachute's cord would be on top instead of down, he'd have the knife to cut the cord to open the parachute properly.

In the military, there would be no haven of security. The air force or pilots never underscored how critical the safe-haven issue was to protect their aircraft the best they could from enemy fire. The gunship played a pivotal role in providing firepower in this campaign. The Spectre gunships are credited with saving the lives of many friendly personnel. The Hercules holds the record for the largest and heaviest aircraft to land on an aircraft carrier. In 1963, the aircraft landed on the USS *Forrester.*

The AC-130 serves today as the main airlift for many military forces worldwide. For nearly fifty years, it is one of the only military aircraft to remain in continuous production with the United States Air Force. Over forty models and variants were deployed to bases worldwide serving with more than sixty nations. Harry flew five of the C-130 models: C-130B, C-130E, AC-130A, AC-130E, and AC-130H. Although the aircraft had project names, they were commonly referred by the squadron as Spectre. The Lockheed AC-130 Spectre gunship is a heavily armed ground-attack variant of the A-130 Hercules transport plane.

Harry always flew out solo; he never flew in formation. Harry was assigned different missions during World War II than during Vietnam. He experienced flak in World War II, but it was Vietnam that was the worst. Harry says, "Those old gunships were after us all the time. Of course, we did a lot of damage, and they were after us."

The AC-130H crew of fourteen consisted of pilot, copilot, navigator, fire officer, electric warfare officer, fight engineer, loadmaster, operators for TV, infrared detection set, and five aerial gunners. The earlier C-130 consisted of a ten-member crew.

Chapter Eight

Major Role of Different Aircrafts

Looking ahead into the future, Gen. H. H. "Hap" Arnold USAAF, V-J Day 1945, stated:

> *The next war may be fought by airplanes with no men in them at all . . . Take everything you've learned about aviation in war, throw it out of the window, and let's go to work on tomorrow's aviation.*

General Arnold held the grades of general of the army and general of the air force. He is the only air force general to hold five-star and the only person to hold a five-star rank in two different US military services.

During Harry's time of serving in the United States Army Air Forces and United States Air Force, he experienced mass production of aircraft. He flew some forty-three different aircraft while in the air force, such as the Curtiss C-46 Commando, a transport aircraft designed at Curtiss-Wright. The aircraft was given name such as the Whale and the Curtiss Calamity by those that flew the aircraft. Nevertheless, the aircraft played a major role in both Europe and the Pacific operations. At the time of its first production, it was the largest twin-engine aircraft in the world and largest and heaviest twin-engine to see major action in World War II. The C-46 originally derived from a commercial high-altitude airliner design. Strato-Freight Curtiss Wright aircraft was a troop carrier and had cargo-paratroop doors on both sides of the fuselage. The D model's nose section was redesigned to incorporate additional radios and flight instruments. After World War II, the marketplace was dominated with the C-46 relegated to primarily cargo duty. While in reserves, Harry flew the C-46 for Reserve Wing, flying for about two years.

The Douglas C-47 Skytrain was used to transport cargo, troops, and wounded armies. It was the best commercial transport aircraft due to its high level of performance during that era. It was used to transport military personnel. The Douglas C-54E Skymaster, a four-engine military transport aircraft used in World War II and the Korean War. Besides transport of cargo, the C-54 also carried presidents, prime ministers, and military staff. In fact, it was the first aircraft to carry the president of the United States and assume the designated name Air Force One.

The Fairchild C-119 Flying Boxcar was used by the air force, navy, and Marine Corps. Its cargo-hauling ability and its unusual appearance earned it the Flying Boxcar nickname. A military transport aircraft designed to carry cargo, personnel, litter patients, and mechanized equipment and to drop cargo and troops by parachute.

EC-135 Looking Glass was a versatile airframe with excellent airspeed, rage, endurance, and air-refueling flexibility. All the EC-135 aircrafts were both tanker receiver and air-refueling capable, which allows it to virtually be self-sufficient. In addition, air refueling allows the aircraft's missions to be extended almost indefinitely, giving it range to conduct nonstop operations to any operating location worldwide. The aircraft was in the air at all times twenty-four hours a day, 365 days a year.

In 1968, Spectre flew its first mission with F-4 fighter escort. A tactic implemented to protect the gunship. Harry would have two (some used three) F-4 Phantom fighter escorts to protect the gunship against heavy and concentrated AAA fire. When Harry went up north and the two escorts fighter planes went to the tanker to get fuel, this left the gunship there alone for the adversary to come out after them. The only thing the gunship's crew could do was go in the timber of night, which was not a good place to be. You can't see, and you don't dare turn on the lights, so they just took a chance out there alone. Harry said, "We got to do different. My crew is not going to have to do that." The fighter pilots said, "Well, we always go to the tanker together." Harry said, "No, you don't!" Harry went and got checked out in the F-4 fighter, and then two of them went up there. The other pilot said, "Let's go get some fuel." Harry said, "Not just *let's* go get some fuel—either *you are going* to go or *I am going* to go to the tanker." The fighter pilot said, "Oh, we always go together." Harry says, "No, we don't. Somebody is going to stay and protect this gunship. If you want to stay or go get some fuel, it is your choice, or I will go and come back, and then you can go." The fighter pilot didn't like it too well. There were some animosity between the pilots of the C-130 gunship and the fighter pilots. After Harry got checked out in the F-4 and set new rules where one fighter would go and come back and then the other would go to the tanker. This way the gunship was getting the support protection needed. Harry said the fighter pilots got where they understood. Although rivalry existed, when on escort duty, the fighter pilots *always* forged flying close to the bomber to *protect* and *escort* home the crippled plane and fend off any enemy fighter looking for prey.

Harry flew F-4 fighter on ten missions, plus eight missions off the carrier. There was a crew of two. The Phantom was the first McDonnell Douglas jet fighter. They were the results of Secretary of Defense Robert McNamara's push to create a unified fighter for all brands of military. With the unification of designations, the Phantom became the F-4. It was a tandem two-seater, twin-engine, all-weather, long-range supersonic jet interceptor fighter bomber. The fighter was developed for the United States Navy, Marine Corps, and the United States Air Force. It was used extensively and became important in the ground attack and reconnaissance during the latter part of the war.

The F-4 fighter first took to guard the skies in May 1958–1962, with top speeds more than twice that of sound. Mach speeds were almost unheard of, and the records were not broken until after the Vietnam War. The fighter had a top speed of Mach 2.23 and an initial climb rate of over 41,000 feet a minute. Like other interceptors of its time, the F-4 was designed without internal cannon. The F-4 was the most versatile fighter ever built. The Phantom fighter earned the distinction of being the last of United States's fighter to attain ace status in the twentieth-century. The miracle was the design in the aircraft.

The fighter arrived in South Vietnam in September 1967 under the Gunship II program and began combat operations over Laos and South Vietnam. The distinction of a fighter is its speed, measurability, and small size relative to other combat aircraft. Innovations in the F-4 included advanced pulse-Doppler radar and extensive use of titanium in its airframe. The numeral II was discontinued to be called plain Phantom in 1959.

The military uses *F* to indicate a fighter plane. Fighter designs are often useful as multirole fighter bombers, strike fighters, and sometimes lighter, fighter-sized tactical ground-attack aircraft used to shoot down other aircraft. The fighter's greatest advantage was its in-air combat that permitted a skilled pilot the liberty to engage and disengage from the fight at his chosen mode of action.

Many of the fighters have secondary ground attack capabilities; some are dual-purpose fighter bombers; a fighter's main purpose is to establish air superiority over a battlefield. American losses were high until the fighter escorts were deployed as a long-range fighter for supporting the bomber missions. The F-4 became known as one of the most popular multipurpose aircrafts in US history.

Harry says there was a Lt. Col. D. C. Vest with the United States Air Force—Aerial Operations, 336th Tactical Fighter Squadron commander, American—in Thailand, Ubon Royal Thai. He would rotate over to Vietnam for three to six weeks. Lt. Col. D. C. Vest flew one hundred combat missions over North Vietnam by 1972.

While in Vietnam, the general sent Harry out on a mission to save a temple in the Lockheed AC-130E gunship aircraft. The Cambodia commander and Harry had worked out a plan. Harry had a box in his airplane, and the Cambodian commander had his box (same kind); if they looked inside their box, each agreed they didn't have to communicate. With the North Vietnamese listening, then they couldn't interrupt what Harry and the commander were saying. They didn't know the location of where the communication was coming from in Europe for there was a lot of aircraft in the air.

Harry was trying to find out if the North Vietnamese troops were up by Angkor Wat, an archaeological site in northwest Cambodia and capital of the Khmer Empire. If they were up there, they could destroy the area. The Cambodian commander backed off his troops so Harry could go along there and go after them. Harry went up there; the gunship had this big gun with 150-mm artillery cannon and started dropping bombs that had little nails and stuff in them at five hundred feet and let them go. Of course, there was nothing going to live down there on the ground; it just pulverized around five hundred feet. There were 3,049 people killed. Harry says, "I am not sure if I should be proud of that or not. I saved the commander's troops, the Angkor Wat, and Cambodia."

Angkor Wat is the largest Hindu temple in the world. Cambodia is the home to one of the only two temples dedicated to Brahma in the world. For this mission, Harry was given the highest Vietnamese congregational award. Cambodia was a lonely planet; its tiny army never stood a chance. King Sihanuok of Cambodia allowed the United States and South Vietnam to enter Cambodia in their fight against communism.

While out on an assigned mission in Vietnam, a big missile went off right beside Harry up there about six hundred feet, hitting the vertical sterilizer on one side and knocking out the windshield and badly damaging the aircraft. "If the missile had gone off down below," says Harry, "I wouldn't have survived. There was a crew of eighteen. It killed three in the back of the aircraft. The navigator would locate the targets and then put me on the targets. The crew was loading ammunition while trying to look over and see if someone is shooting at you all the while flying in an ice storm, trying to keep from getting hit. Sometimes you get hit anyway. I was able to get the aircraft back."

When they had night shooting, Harry said they'd put on their jacket and hat and go out and shoot down at night. They had to work with the navigation people for there were a lot of ships out there at nights, and they didn't want us shooting at their ships.

Harry had eighteen AC-130 gunships in Vietnam at one time and over six thousand people working. He lost one gunship and another the day he left, and two more of the gunships were lost later. Harry had trained all the crewmen. It is hard when you know them but even harder as commander to notify the families. Being a father of two sons and one of them a United States Air Force pilot didn't make it any easier task. They were young men going to college or just out of high school when they entered the military. Most of them had volunteered.

While in Thailand, the noncommissioned black officers had a place downtown. It was a bar. The two-star general came through and said he had heard a lot about the place and asked Harry how many times he had been down there, and Harry said, "Never." The general said, "Don't you think you ought to?" Harry said, "Okay!" Harry called and told them that he was coming down tonight, and they said, "Good, I will meet you at the door!" Harry put on his best clothes and called the security military police to drive him down there and wait. Harry said, "In there it seemed like there were four hundred people, but there probably wasn't. They had a table set up right in the center. I had a good time, it was a nice place. Everyone was receptive. The general didn't want me to tell him that, but it was true. You know, that helped all those guys. I'd gone sooner had I known. I always had a lot of paperwork. I went a time or two."

Harry never drank anything, for he never knew when he may be called to fly a mission. He had to be prepared and ready at all times. As for officers, just because they are officers, that doesn't mean they can't get smashed.

There was a big black fella, a chief master sergeant, in charge of the gunners on Harry's aircraft. Most gunners were black. He must have weighed 220 pounds. His wife came over while he was assigned at Bangkok, Thailand, to visit. She said she wanted to see Colonel Canham and went to meet him. She was about as big as her husband. Harry said, "I never got such a big hug in my life. The girls went on a little trip together. They always like to go shopping. She tried to think of something to get me. She came to see me before she left and brought a gift. I got another big hug. She stayed about a month. She was nice . . . a very sincere person."

During the time the black lady visited Thailand, Harry's wife was also there for around ten days. It was the first time that Harry had anyone to visit him in an operating zone.

On the day Harry lost the *first* one of his AC-130 gunships, Harry's mother called his wife, Betty, telling her that Harry had lost a gunship. Harry had not called and *never* knew that his mother had called his wife until he called her the next morning. When he told Betty, she said, "I know, your mother called and told me last night." Harry told Betty, "I never called her."

Although her son was beyond arms' reach, Harry's mother had felt that sense of him having lost a gunship. Many times, mothers have the gift to possess this sense to predict, sense through strong feelings that something will happen just before it does or at the time it occurs. It is a God-given gift for some.

The chaplain where Harry went to church told Harry he didn't know what it was that they did. Harry said he would take him out sometime with him; the chaplain was all for going along. Harry told him that he would take him out that night. When they went down to get their equipment to go, Harry told the chaplain to get a gun. The chaplain said, "Oh! I can't shoot that." Harry told him he'd need it if they were shot down and to get food with, and he said, "I can do that!"

The Pacific Squadron Head Command Chaplain got wind of it and came down to check and see if Harry had ordered the chaplain to go. Harry said he didn't, and the Squadron Head Command chaplain, knowing Harry, said everything was okay and visited. The chaplain said going out with Harry was one of the best things he'd ever done. Harry gave the chaplain a firsthand experience of what *it was* that he and his group did. Colonel Canham's mission was to fly, fight, and win. To pilot one of the most advanced aircrafts required extraordinary skill and precision.

North American, Boeing, McDonnell Douglas, and Lockheed have turned out superior aircraft. The jet aviation advances have been phenomenal. After World War II, understandably, Harry could foresee how the social effect that commercial jet aircraft would revolutionized the world, opening up every corner of the world through commercial aviation. Looking into the future as General H. H. "Hap" Arnold, USAAF, had stated in 1945, Harry knew new advanced technologies will continue to inspire aviation's future of tomorrow. The jet age has shaped our country just as the car has become a crucial part of our nation.

Chapter Nine

USAF Secretary Robert Seamans

The Sixteenth Special Operations Squadron accomplished some amazing feats during the Southeast Asia tour as the most deadly night-flying weapons system in the theater. The AC-130s destroyed and participated in many crucial close air fire support platform with outstanding capabilities; with extremely accurate fire control system, the AC-130 could place 20-mm, 40-mm, 105-mm on target with first round accuracy. The AC-130 gunship earned a reputation as one of the deadliest combat weapons on the planet, *transport plane with power*. On missions, Harry did all the firing on the Martin B-26 Marauder and C-130 gunships.

Harry was presented with the Distinguished Flying Cross on 16 January 1972. On that date, while participating on a night armed reconnaissance mission as an AC-130 gunship pilot over Southeast Asia, his actions led to the damage and destruction of twelve hostile supply vehicles and the ignition of numerous secondary fires and explosions and succeeded in destroying large amounts of supplies and munitions. In the face of twenty-two rounds of hostile antiaircraft fire, undaunted, Harry continued the assault. Amidst the heroism during that time of the action displayed by Col. Harry Canham, there were immediate and telling results of courage and self-sacrifice. Harry never once put his personal safety upfront of completing the mission. It was a reflection of his competence, aerial skill, and devotion to duty.

There were always targets in Vietnam to defend. One night, Harry was called to help in Laotian against the North Vietcong targets that were too much for the Laotian's equipment. Harry, flying his gunship, went in and destroyed a big tank with the 105 mm. The next day, he was presented with the tank entrance lid by Jimmy Nichols, VC commander and Laotian general.

Harry flew several different aircraft while serving the air force. Another bomber aircraft Col. Harry Canham flew was the Douglas A-20G Havoc; it was an American lightweight attack intruder and night fighter aircraft during World War II. It was extremely adaptable and played a major role in every combat theater of the war. It became known as a pilot's favorite aircraft of the war due to the ability to pitch it around like a fighter.

The Douglas A-26 Invader that was designed during 1948 through 1965. A United States twin-engine light bomber and attack aircraft. It was a fast aircraft capable of carrying twice its specified bomb load. To produce a formidable ground-attack aircraft, it could be fitted with a range of guns.

Harry flew three models of the North American B-25A Mitchell *Barbie III* bomber. It was a two-engine medium bomber named in honor of military pioneer Gen. Billy Mitchell. General Mitchell is regarded as the Father of the United States Air Force. General Mitchell served the United States Army from 1898 to 1926.

The pilot and copilot and bombardier were provided with armor behind their seats of the bomber. North American B-25H Mitchell *Barbie III*, the successor to the B-25Gs, was designed with more horsepower. The B-25G model was developed with the standard-length transparent nose, and the bombardiers were replaced by a shorter solid nose containing guns and cannon. Harry also flew the last B-25J version that looked much like the earlier B, C, and D that had been reverted to the longer glazed bombardier nose, but with the H version's relocated forward dorsal manned turret. The B-25 plane is well remembered for the Doolittle Raid on 18 April 1942, the first air raid of World War II by the United States to strike the Japanese homeland. The B-25 became a symbol of American airpower during World War II. They were the heaviest aircraft at the time to be flown from a ship at sea and the most well-known bombers from World War II, a favorite of many pilots for its flying ability and easy landing.

Harry flew both the E and G models of the Boeing B-17 Flying Fortress, a four-engine heavy bomber. When he went to England after the war, there was a B-17 over there that they used to back up the general. The general came down one day, and the B-17 was just setting. He said, "Use it a little bit. It is not good for it to be sitting, waiting for me."

There was a colonel that had been flying it and got checked out in it. Harry had him to check him out in it, and they spent quite a bit of time flying the B-17. The aircraft was a potent, high-flying, long-range bomber. The B-17E model was the first model primarily focused on warfare. The Boeing B-17Gs were the most numerous of the B-17s models. The B-17G was one of the first finished model airplanes to roll off the assembly line. The G model sported the defenses firepower of thirteen Browning .50 caliber machine guns from the regional seven. The B-17Gs were designed five inches shorter than the earlier version. The B-17G was the final version of the Flying Fortress. The B17s first carried a crew of ten and later in the war dropped to a nine crew. The aircraft was primarily employed by the United States Army Air Forces in the daylight bombing campaign against German industrial and military targets. It was a very trustworthy aircraft. Many of the B-17Gs were converted after the wars' end for other missions as cargo hauling, engine testing, reconnaissance, and search-and-rescue duties. The close formation alone did not prove effective, and the bombers were given fighter escorts to operate successfully.

Aerial bombardment became a more important factor for the Allied winning of the war and protecting the ground troops. World War II airmen fought flying in the air over land and sea, over several diverse theaters of operation to protect and defend their country—selflessly sacrificing their own lives.

When Harry returned from Vietnam for the last time and went to London, his name was put on the promotion list for one-star. The list was sent to Congress for approval, and they threw out Harry's name because he was *too* old. The Congress members said, "If you had your fiftieth birthday, you won't be promoted. A whole lot of you get your promotion and stay in one year and retire and take that money."

As it turned out for Harry, it was more beneficial that he retired at the rank he had because of the new policy change. Harry would get three hundred dollars more than if he'd retired the month before at a rank promotion. Harry had just fallen into the new policy change, which was a miracle. Harry was quite qualified to be promoted to one-star rank. Age should not have played a part in Congress's decision with Harry's service record.

Harry met different generals throughout his service time. In 1972, Dr. Robert Channing Seamans, Jr., secretary of the United States Air Force visited the Ubon, Thailand, air force base. Colonel Canham showed Dr. Seamans the AC-130 gunship and talked with him about the firing power of the cannons.

NASA administrator Michael Griffin stated of Dr. Robert Seamans who died in 2008:

> *Robert Seamans was one of the early leaders in launching NASA's efforts to explore the new frontier of space. As NASA's associate administrator and then deputy administrator, Bob, as top manager and consummate engineer was instrumental in the decision-making, planning, and program execution that enabled the United States to meet President Kennedy's goal of landing men on the Moon. He will be remembered as one of the great pioneers and leaders of America's space program.*

In 1960, Dr. Seamans joined NASA as an associate administrator and then as deputy administrator from 1965 to 1968. He served as the ninth secretary of the United States Air Force from 15 February 1969 to May 1973. He was appointed by President Richard Nixon.

Dr. Robert Seamans's legacy will live on in the many different capacities that he so honorably served, working with presidents to lead the nation's space program from its infancy to its triumph. He was instrumental in the decision to send Apollo 8 to the moon, which paved the way for the lunar landing. John Glenn became the first man to orbit the earth in 1962. He circled the planet three times in his Mercury *Friendship 7* spaceship. Neil Armstrong is the first man to set foot on the moon in 1969. Dr. Seamans worked closely with President Kennedy's administration toward achieving his pledge of a manned lunar landing by the end of the decade. He was a man that *never* let problems stand in the way of achieving a daunting task that would change and define America. Harry served with ten different secretaries of air force from 1947 to 1974.

Harry Canham's first air forces cap.

Short snorter (one-dollar bill).

Summer of 1943, trainer airplane over city of Dennison, Texas, in background.

World War II Martin B-26 Marauder (Photo: RMP Archive/Lorathea Lange)

Curtiss C-46 Commando North Africa, 1945.

7,509th Operations Squadron passing reviewing stand; Captain Harry G. Canham, A0-702234, commanding, 1948 or 1949.

Douglas C-124 Globemaster II heavy-lift military transport and the largest aircraft in the United States Air Force.

Douglas C-124 atomic weapons carrier and capable of carrying 425 people, which was classified until 2000.

Gen. Walter C. Sweeney, Jr., a United States Air Force four-star general, who served as USAF Tactical Air commander at Langley AFB, Virginia. Years of service at Tactical Air Command, 1930–1965.

Col. Harry Canham and son Michael. Picture taken in June 1970 at Michael's graduation from officer training school (OTC). Michael's mother, Betty, with his father attended his graduation ceremony.

Cmdr. Col. Harry G. Canham, 777 Tactical Airlift Squadron, Pope Air Force Base, North Carolina, 1970.

Cmdr. Col. Harry Canham at desk—AC-130 gunships, Ubon, Thailand, 1972.

Cmdr. Col. Harry Canham, AC-130 gunships, Ubon airfield, Thailand, 1972.

Col. Harry Canham preparing for an F-4 Phantom night mission, 1972.

Col. Canham, Ubon, Thailand, getting in F-4 Phantom, 1972.

L-R: Pacific commanding general and Cmdr. Canham of AC-130 gunships, 1972.

Jimmy Nichols, VC Cmdr., (*center*) and Laotian general (*right*) presenting at headquarters Colonel Canham (*left*) with a tank entrance lid that he had destroyed the night before in Laos, 1972.

AC-130 gunship on takeoff, 1972.

L-R: Cmdr. Col. Canham, commander of AC-130 gunship, and Dr. Robert Channing Seamans, Jr., secretary of United States Air Force (1969–1972), Ubon, Thailand.

Inside AC-130 gunship 105 mm.

AC-130 gunship—20-mm cannons, 1972.

20-mm guns on AC-130 gunship.

AC-130 105 mm on gunship, 1972.

AC-130 night flares, 1972.

AC-130, Vietnam battle damage, Col. Canham, pilot, 1972.

AC-130, Vietnam battle damage, Col. Canham, 1972.

AC-130, Vietnam battle damage, Col. Canham, pilot, 1972.

B-17G Flying Fortress. Harry flew this aircraft in England, but not in any missions. Picture by author, Ruby Gwin, at a B-7G Overcast Show at Purdue University, August 2013. Aircraft was flown by Rick Fernald and Ken Morris.

Rick Fernald of Yelm, Washington, flew a tour in Guam and one in Thailand, supporting air operations in Southeast Asia. He served with the 441st Bomb Squadron and the 320th Bomb Wing. Ken Morris flew for both Delta and Northwest Airlines. He is owner of the Taildragger Aviation business in Northern Illinois, on the Poplar Grove Airport (C77).

Billy G. Gilmore, MSgt., USAF (Ret.).

L-R: Sgt. Billy Gilmore—men talking unknown.

Lt. Mike Canham on a step of Northrop T-38 Talon supersonic trainer jet at Vance AFB, Enid, Oklahoma, May 1971.

Lt. Mike Canham, March 1972.

Harry, Marc, and Betty Canham—Marc's graduation from UCA, Conway, Arkansas, 1976.

L-R: Capt. Mike Canham with Col. Dick Bladder, Korean DMZ, March 1982.

Chapter Ten

Aviators' Mission Ends

Returning from Vietnam in 1973, Harry returned to his family in Sherwood, Arkansas, for thirty days, the only thirty-day leave of his air force career. He then was assigned deputy director of Airlift Headquarters, TAC, Langley Air Force Base, Virginia, in January 1973. Harry left Sherwood for the assignment before the New Year. Later in July, he was assigned director of Airlift Headquarters, TAC, Langley Air Force Base in Virginia.

At last, it was time for Harry to say good-bye to the United States Air Force. Missions accomplished. He had done his part in the military, so now, it is home to a new and different life; the air force had been his home for thirty-two years. What an honorable record that Harry had built. He gave purely, knowing war does ask courage of men but also does peace. Shrouded by wartime secrecy, this incredible story of Col. Harry Canham's top secret official military files are most meaningful, a poignant memory.

Harry flew over different continents on classified missions, and in that came honor; for Harry that was honor enough. He never let fear in; he always faced a dangerous mission with courage. Harry's character of nature is to *never give up*. During his time of service, he earned many medals and decorations, but his main objective was to *fly* and *protect*.

It was over! In 1974, Col. Harry Canham retired from the air force and returned to Sherwood, Arkansas. Harry left behind a chronicle mission record of significance—tales of courage. Sadly, those many papers, records, sheets, and personal belongings were lost on his movement back to Sherwood, which was a valuable loss. Those chronological air force tree branches Harry had built were records that represented the spirit and ideals of the heart of a young man making a decision back in December 1941. In those records were lost data information of aerial skill, duty, devotion, and honorable deeds.

Harry saw aircrafts go through several alterations in each of their design stages and variants, and engineers continued to improve their aircraft's effectiveness upon the basic design. The process helped along with the cadet experience and was a vital link to mold the pilots of the United States Air Force. Fighters, bombers, and transport played deciding roles in the outcome in the European and Pacific theaters during World War II. Aircraft was a major part of Harry's life, having flown so many during his military years. Pilots had a preference for aircraft. For Harry, all the C-130 gunship versions are his favorite aircraft.

Harry flew under commanders' orders, and many times, ahead of a mission, Harry would be notified after a short briefing and go straight to the airplane. For Harry, there was meaning in his job; he loved flying. To fly was a powerful lure; he didn't fly for worldwide recognition but to fly, fight, and to obey the laws of war. His top secret missions took place away from any operational publicity because of their nature. While in the cockpit, he always flew with his tools of faith, concentration and laser focus, with alertness and respect for the US Air Force core values: "Integrity first," "Service before self," "Excellence in all we do," and "To get a mission done."

Harry *never* mentions any unpredictability that came with being a pilot. Of his time in the air force, Harry said, "I have fond memories, supporting my commander in chief, the president, and completing all jobs assigned me, moving weapons, standing alert and defending peace, and taking my turn going to war and doing my best to see that we would win *whatever* the cost."

While Harry and comrades were serving on two warfronts, America was serving in the fight here with home-front support. It was a war that united America with a common purpose. As did Harry's parents, everyone worked long hours. Rationing was introduced on certain things because of the supply shortage; rationing books helped to make sure everyone got their fair share. Like today, you couldn't just walk into a store and buy all you wanted of sugar, coffee, or meat. The president called on citizens to help by contributing scrap rubber. The rubber situation was the worst. Rubber items became the first nonfood item to be rationed. The Japanese had seized plantations in the Dutch East Indies that produced 90 percent of America's raw rubber. The steel industry rapidly stepped up its production; drives were geared up to collect all old scrap iron and aluminum products to melt down for use. On the home front was displayed a WPA poster: Salvage Scrap to Beat the Japs.

Gas was rationed, which meant you could only purchase what your classification ration sticker allowed. Rationing hit the farmers from equipment to other needs as fencing. Farmers became known as America's foot soldiers working to protect from home as sons, fathers, and grandfathers were fighting on foreign soil.

There was a surmountable four-year effort during World War II on foreign soil, in the air, on land, and at home. There were US war bond drives during World War II to help fund the wartime efforts to support our boys in trenches, on water and air. The drives used celebrities to promote the bonds, along with poster advertising drives using different slogans. America had given its all know-how and energy; it was incredible. There was a staggering amount of dollars spent to fight World War II. Those drives were not revived during the Korean and Vietnam wars. As one of the wartime slogans read, "We're all in it together," proved it does take a *patriotic village* to win. Our young people have no understanding of the magnitude of the legacy that remains timeless. America would never be the same. The United States rescued Europe with billions of dollars in 1948. The Marshall Plan saved Europe for democracy.

For Harry, he had seen and had experienced some comical things during his military days. He was in a meeting, and this Turkish general's English was not too good and kind of slurred around with Major Canham's "*so use-a-ful help.*" Harry's general turned around and lowered his glasses. Harry said, "They got a chuckle out of that. I would never have said *so use-a-ful.*"

Harry played a major part in the war strategy through helping with long-term planning to guarantee security through *displaying tactics* and through *military strategy*, especially methods that were employed and directed to secure through *aircraft*, *weapons*, and *contributions* in the field of operations. At times, it was hard for Harry to talk about his military experiences. To look back and talk of lost friends and innocent people was hard. Harry will tell humorous experiences in between to help tell his story. There is nothing more riveting than to meet and talk with a pilot who willingly took personal flight risks, knowing that it may be his last.

Seeing his face light up when he talks about an aircraft, one gets a feel of the full extent of Harry's 22,000 hours in the air. Whenever a friend brings Harry all new information released on the C-130 gunships, he says, "My goodness, it is awesome of the new equipment that they are putting on them."

While overseas, Harry recalled, they had a situation that could have left dire consequences and a decision had to be made before a real tragedy occurred. A young fella went out and got in an aircraft and took it up flying around. He wasn't a pilot, but he knew how to fly the aircraft. While in cadet training, the young fella was a model cadet.

The area that the enlisted airman was flying around was heavily populated, and if he crashed, it would have done a lot of damage and kill innocent people. He wouldn't respond to their call in. The Army Air Forces realized what they were dealing with and had to make a prompt decision of what to do. It was decided to shoot the aircraft down. There was no other way to alter or adapt a way to get the young airman at the controls down. Such decisions come hard to make. One never knows what possesses a person to do what they sometimes do.

It was twice more dangerous for a cadet to learn and get into combat than it was to actually fly the assigned mission. The Army Air Forces World War II fatalities were high. About one-third of trainees were killed in training crashes, one-third to operational accidents and one-third to enemy combat. United States Army Air Forces incurred 12 percent of the army's 936,000 battle casualties in World War II. Total sorties flown by the United States Army Air Forces during World War II were 2,352,800, with 1,693,565 of them flown in Europe-related areas and 669,235 flown in the Pacific and Far East.

On January 1973, the Vietnam peace accord went into effect; the Spectre operations ended in Vietnam. Spectre remained active in the region, supporting operations in Laos and Cambodia until 1973. American offensive operations in Laos ended, and the gunship became committed to the Cambodian conflict operation. In 1962, President Kennedy was convinced that the pro-United States regime in South Vietnam simply could not beat the insurgents and planned to withdraw a thousand United States troops by the end of 1963. On hindsight that decision was right, but with the president's assassination, those plans were not kept. Vietnam, from Harry's standpoint, was one long, tough fought war. He says Vietnam War was hard to explain.

It was long and more painful struggle than later generation would understand or sufficiently appreciate the contribution our boys gave—not an outcome of a miracle. World War II left our country with its head held high, where the Vietnam War was left without a less certain moral compass. American air power played a decisive role for the North Vietnamese to return to peace negotiations and quickly concluded a settlement in ending the long conflict. Regretfully, our soldiers came home to be spit on and shunned—not to open arms, but to see their country turn their backs. Our country *must* focus on *never* letting another soldier be treated as our Vietnam soldiers. They were men sent off to war, answering to our nation's call to defend. May the world continue to search for means of achieving peace and security by following the principles of peace, freedom, and justice.

Chapter Eleven

Home's New Calling

Today, Harry lives close to the Little Rock Air Force Base, where he served and trained pilots. The air base would continue to play a major role in Harry's civilian life. When Harry was training at the Little Rock Air Force Base, they didn't have enough landing space and needed more. He talked to the general, and he said, "Why don't you go over to the Little Rock airport and see what they say."

Harry called the airport manager, and he couldn't have been nicer. Harry went out to meet the manager, and they went up to his office and had coffee and whatever snack they wanted. The manager was excited about Harry's plan. He said, "You know, we can't keep up our jurisdiction for approach landings and have to hire new people all the time because we have so many to keep up their qualifications.

Harry told him, "We will train your people. We'll get them all qualified the first week, for that is how many we can do." The airport manager fell in love with the plan. Harry got the entire airport's people qualified, and they still see nineties over there. They worked together all the time. If they happen to get busy, the air force people broke traffic and let them go and come back in. There was aircraft flying all the time from the air force base and Little Rock airport. Thus, it proved that despite differences between civilian and military, something could be made to work by talking.

Harry volunteered at the Little Rock Air Force Retiree Activities Office and the Little Rock Air Force Base Clinic Pharmacy for thirty years, handing out refill prescriptions, once they were filled, to customers one day a week. The refill pharmacy is totally staffed with volunteers. Harry volunteered with good friend, Lt. Col. Allen Hamman of Sherwood, Arkansas. Allen Hamman died in 2012. Harry plays a low-profile and a lack of awareness of the truly outstanding achievements of his thirty-two years of military and thirty-years of civilian volunteering service. To serve in various theaters on diverse aircrafts on multiple missions and on the Little Rock Air Force Base was a very natural thing for Harry.

As an avid skeet shooter, Harry enjoys going out to the skeet club and practice shooting with his twenty and ten gauge. He always enjoyed going hunting and still has the hunting knife he used as a young boy in Wataga, Illinois. Going out and unleashing his hunting and skeet shooting skills has always been a meaningful sport for Harry.

Harry started the skeet club at the Little Rock Air Force Base. Due to the use of guns, the club was moved from the base to two other locations before they found a permanent location. When Michael is home, sometimes he goes with his father out to the skeet club field and shoots. Michael said, "Between the fact that we are both air force pilots and we both shoot skeet, we have always had that between us. We have shot skeet over fifty years."

Harry had two sons, Marc Alan and Michael Harry. Marc was unable to pass the military medical test, but Michael would follow his father's military profession after graduating from Bradley University in Peoria, Illinois. His father attended his graduation, not wanting to draw attention to himself, but all his medals did just that!

As second generation, Michael volunteered for the air force. When he graduated from flying school, Harry got the honor pinning the wings on Michael, a special moment for father and son. Michael would also fly cargo aircraft and Northrop T-38 Talon fighter jets. The T-38 Talon is a two-seater, twin-engine supersonic jet trainer. The T-38 was the world's first supersonic trainer and the most produced. The United

States Air Force operates the T-38s to train United States Air Force pilots and is also used by NASA.

Later, Michael served as flight instructor at Maxwell Air Force Base, Montgomery, Alabama. The home of one of our nation's most prestigious air bases that dates back to the Wright Brother's flying school. It is a United States Air Force installation under the Air Education and Air Force center for Professional and Training Command (AETC).

Michael retired as an air force captain in 1990. He would continue in navigation, just as his father, after he retired from the air force. Michael flew Learjet 60 for a bank holding company in Birmingham, Alabama. He was chief pilot for them from 1990 to 2006. Michael and his wife, Gwen, bought a motor coach, forty-three-foot long Allegro Bus and have traveled for the past eight years. They spend their winters in Florida.

After Michael completed air force pilot school, his father was the director of operations at Little Rock Air Force Base. One afternoon, Michael was on leave, visiting his parents, and Michael went out with his father and flew on a training mission. His father in the *left* command seat on a United States Air Force C-130 and Michael in the *right* seat or copilot seat; they flew three instrument approaches. When Michael was the chief pilot for South Trust, he just happened to stop for fuel on his way to take the Learjet 60 for maintenance, and his father and Carlyn joined Michael and his copilot for lunch at the Little Rock airport. Michael asked his copilot to sit in the rear with Carlyn, and they flew around the local area for about an hour. This time, it was Michael in the *left* seat and his father in the *right*. Michael had his father to take the controls. With all that *awesome new equipment*, Harry flew the Learjet 60 that he had never flown. The Learjet 60 is a medium-range business jet aircraft manufactured by Bombardier Aerospace in Wichita, Kansas. The Learjet is notable for its time-to-climb performance of 41,000 feet in 68.5 minutes. It was a pivotal occasion for Michael. He got to see that his father's flying knowledge at the controls was sharp as ever. It had been thirty years since Harry had flown any aircraft. With the many changes made on aircrafts, his father adapted right off to flying the Learjet as if he'd remembered it like yesterday. It was a memorable time for son and father. Michael said, "An experience I will *never* forget."

Chapter Twelve

Civilian Life

While Harry was director of operations at the Little Rock Air Force Base, the Wing Commander set up then was wing commander, director of material, and director of operations. When the wing commander was gone and with maintenance not on flying status, that left Harry to wing command with him being on flying status. Harry got to winging; he signed in, and as soon as that was done, the wing commander took off for thirty days, leaving Harry to wing command.

In civilian life, Harry immediately propelled to continue on a journey that returns him with navigation. He started flying for British Air Space. He flew for them for five years. Harry then went to Decatur, Illinois, where he helped build a building with BorgWarner Incorporation. BorgWarner is a worldwide company serving nineteen countries. The company was best known as the supplier of Warner Gear overdrive units for cars of the 1930s to the 1970s. The company provided drivetrain components to all three United States automakers, as well as a variety of European and Asian. The company was a developer of Ford's Ford-O-Matic three-speed automatic transmission introduced in 1950, along with "Holly" brand Borg and Beck carburetors. The BorgWarner Indianapolis 500 racing event has been provided by BorgWarner since 1936. The structure was two key business divisions: Engine Group and Drivetrain Group. BorgWarner is also known for its ownership of the Norge Appliance Company of washer and dryers.

When Harry came back from Decatur, Illinois, British Air Space called and said they would like for him to come out and work. Harry said, "I don't think so."

They said, "Now, we are going to pay you more money. Can you come out and look at the job?" Harry said, "Yes, I will come out and look for a little bit and see."

The next morning, Harry went out to British Air Space, and they offered him double the money. They had eighteen used airline twin-engine jets that the British Airlines had turned back with no way to get rid of them. Harry's job was to get them in shape to sell, which was not that hard for Harry. During his assignment in Africa, pilots worked on aircraft; everyone was a mechanic. They worked late into the evening carrying out repairs on aircraft. As for the jets, Harry knew they were run down to nothing but fixable. Harry told them, "Okay."

Harry had to work with the FAA (Federal Aviation Administration) and everything to comply with set regulations. He worked cleaning them and doing all the necessary restorations. He took out seats and carpets and replaced them and did all the necessary painting to get them ready to sale. The British Air Space man in Washington and senior manager of the United States called in and said he was coming down to see what was being done. He was pleased with what he saw and told Harry he was doing a good job. He said, "The only thing, you are not getting paid enough, I am going to double your salary."

The man from Washington was the senior man, so it was his call, not at the local level. Every airplane was sold. People scooped them up. Turbojets, whatever they wanted. A couple of companies bought two or three of them, but it was mostly individuals that bought them. They were aircraft that just needed maintenance.

During this time, Harry's wife, Betty, was quiet ill and died. Harry would later meet and marry the lovely, Carlyn Stark, thirteen years ago. Carlyn's husband, Dr. Bert Stark, Jr., died in 1999. Dr. Stark was a retired professor at the University of Central Arkansas, Conway, Arkansas.

Carlyn has two sons, Dr. R. Lee and Marsha Hinson of Little Rock, Arkansas, and Dr. C. Wallace and Jennifer Hinson of Atlanta, Georgia. Lee has two children, Alex and Katherine. Wally has two children, Katie and Josh, and grandchildren, Nick and Ella. There are two stepsons, Dr. B. Bert and Cornelia Stark and Larry and Claudine Stark; grandson Matt and granddaughters, Laura Marlee and Hailey; and great-granddaughter, Isla Kate.

Carolyn Johnson became a part of the Canham family March 1998. She started taking care of Harry's wife, Betty. After Betty's death, she continued taking care of the house. She works four days a week and at other times if she is needed. She has been a blessing and very dependable.

After surgery in 2008, Harry was presented with a prayer afghan throw by volunteers from the First Methodist Church, Jacksonville, Arkansas. The Methodist Church women knit and crochet afghan throws for missionary service. Before delivering the afghan, the women went up before the pastor, lay the afghan on their left arm, and he gave a prayer. The volunteers are from Harry and Carlyn's church.

Harry and Carlyn live in Sherwood, Arkansas. Harry was a past master of the Masonic Lodge and a member since he was twenty-one. They are active at the University of Central Arkansas in Conway, Arkansas, Carlyn's alma mater and where she served on the alumni board. They enjoy going to the football games and tailgating with friends during the home games. Carlyn says Harry is a very careful driver. When they go somewhere with friends, they always want Harry to drive. In driving a car, for Harry, safety is top priority just as it was with his aircraft crew. Harry is not only a good driver, but son Michael says he is a great cook.

Chapter Thirteen

Old Glory Flies High

There were seventeen in Harry's high school graduation class. Two classmates were killed in combat, and one was captured and died in captivity. One of them had volunteered along with Harry. The other friend Lawrence Giddings would later die of cancer. For Harry Canham, he made it home but not unscratched. After he was injured, it never entered his mind to quit and continued to fly eighty-six more missions. Harry's leap of faith he took in late 1941 to volunteer for the United States Army Air Corps to serve his country he says, "I loved my job. Every day you woke up, it was a new deal—challenging!"

Harry met German, Japanese, Italian, and Vietnam military personnel. When asked what he thought of them during the war, he had only one comment: my job was to kill the enemy, and I did that as best I could.

The day Harry received his wings and second lieutenant commission was a *special* day. He never knew what to expect when he entered the military. He never knew the air force was touted as being such an elite outfit. Young men like Harry were idealistic, and he lived up to respecting the training he received. To climb up into his plane to fly a mission, Harry was proud to serve his country. He was molded by the United States Army Air Corps and United States Air Force and has a great respect for the uniform. Col. Harry Canham is a humble person, burning with patriotic zeal.

With great vigor, loyalty, and courage, Harry flew the skies, defending. He flew tirelessly to make the path before him bright as an experienced veteran pilot that met many challenges. He says, "Would I go to war to protect my country? You bet! I will go as long as I live."

There is a retired master sergeant Billy D. Gilmore, MSAF, a flight engineer who lives in Arkansas that flew missions with Harry. Every time Billy sees Harry, he'll say, "Colonel, do you think we have two or three more missions in us?

Sergeant Gilmore, as a member of Harry's flight crew, was the person who monitored and operated the aircraft systems. He, therefore, was an integrated member of the flight deck crew who worked close coordination with Harry and the copilot during all phases of flight. Billy was with Harry in Vietnam and at Little Rock, Arkansas, air force base. The flight engineer position had a specialized control panel, allowing for the monitoring and control of various aircraft systems. Today the aircraft systems are both monitored and adjusted by electronic microprocessors and computers, resulting in the elimination of the flight engineer's position.

Billy said, "One thing that was funny while on a ground force mission at the French Michelin Rubber Plantation. They wanted Harry and crew to shoot through the gunship windows so they wouldn't destroy the area so bad."

The Michelin Rubber Plantation is located approximately halfway between the Cambodian border and Saigon. It was the largest rubber plantation in Vietnam.

In Saigon, the radio radar control was hit. The crew were all lucky, for it was just one of many times the aircraft was hit. They were just lucky to make it home.

While at the Ubon, Thailand, base one morning, Billy said the major asked Harry where he was going. Harry said he was going down to decoupling engine gauges on the AC-130. Billy said that was the way

Harry was. Harry always immersed himself with whatever needed to be done—very dedicated.

Harry has a resolution about him with great integrity. As air commander in Vietnam, his relationship with his brothers-in-arms was one of meriting respect. He valued each that he was assigned over. Many of them at the Arkansas air force base served in Vietnam under Harry. They were all younger. Sergeant Gilmore says of Colonel Canham, "He was great!"

Whenever there was any Distinguished Flying Cross (DFC) medals given on Harry's aircraft, his rule was that *if* anybody was going to get one, they *all* get one. It was not an air force requirement but a rule Harry stuck by on his aircraft. He said, "Everyone was getting shot at and getting hit, not just one. They were not just riding along in the aircraft. There was a master sergeant sitting in between me and my copilot handling the throttle, fuel, and stuff. Sgt. Billy D. Gilmore was as subject to be blown up as I was. He was just as busy as you know what. I'd howler at him for something I wanted on that airplane, and he knew right where to get it. We were used to flying together. That is why I liked to take him. We flew forty to fifty missions together."

Colonel Canham's dedication he displayed for his crewmen defined the pilot he was. He also showed compassion for the people he had come in contact with and had befriended him while flying missions in the many different locations during his military career. Many times he emphasized humanistic values and concerns of what he saw and tried to help. Harry never forgot those good deeds each had given or had shown. He's touched many lives in an extraordinary way with a joyful symbol of humanity and love with a huge force for good.

Some of Harry's *finest hours* were doing what he wanted to do—flying and serving his country. Air force embodied in the air what was always in the forefront. Harry can look back with pride upon the valor of the air force. In all theaters of World War II, air warfare and antiair attack were major components of the United States Army Air Forces. Today our United States Air Force focuses on air and cyberspace superiority and serves as our country's eyes and ears with space satellite, space our whole world operates on. GPS is used by our smartphones, equipment to navigate, and is free to the entire world.

Harry, a sky lover at heart, experienced inspiring heroics of helping to bring peace to the world during its darkest time. Yet today, Harry's curiosity about aircraft has never changed. He keeps up with his beloved gunship changes. The current model of the AC-130 gunship has been used to fight enemy combatants in Iraq, Afghanistan, and Somalia. The United States Air Force is the only user of the AC-130 gunship.

Flying the sky in his gunship was a natural thing for Harry—likened to a spiritual poetry. For thirty-two years, he flew the heavens in the four-engine aircraft, saying, because of their capabilities. Harry has never had to escape from doubt, for he always knew his early desire to fly was the choice that was right for him. He feels honored in that he was given the chance to fly and serve his country. It was never about how many rewards he could earn; it was the depth of commitment of service he could give. Harry will always be bound to his code of conduct oath with the specific pilgrimage of life's course he got to serve. Of his father, Michael said, "My dad is not noted for talking about he has flying experiences in combat. It has been in the last couple of years that he talks about it to me."

Harry remains active at ninety-four with a magnitude of history information. He valued patriotism young; it shaped his outlook on life in a very positive way. Harry is a member of the Arkansas Distinguished Flying Cross (DFC) Society. When he applied for membership, he submitted one DFC, and none of the MOAA (Military Officers Association of America)) society members knew how many Harry really had. After Harry spoke at a 2012 MOAA meeting, there was a question and answer time. One officer asked Harry, "What did you receive your DFC for and how many do you have?"

Harry put his head down and was quiet for a while. He then raised his head, and with tears in his eyes, he said quietly, "I have five Distinguished Flying Crosses."

Colonels present at the MOAA meeting along with Harry were PCINC Col. James D. Elmer, USA (Ret.), Chapter Adjutant Col. Thomas P. Williams, USAF (Ret.), and Lt. Col. Thomas A. Robertson, Jr., USAF (Ret.). Col. James D. Elmer said, "It was a moment I will never forget."

Author's note: I have been fortunate to join a story that is much larger than one person. Reliving Col. Harry Canham's military journey has been unique of a modest man who wished to not tell of his accomplishments, but just a pilot doing his duty. Words simple and unforgettable—Harry knows about military preparedness, global strategy, and combined operations in the coalition war against fascism waged in the air over several diverse theaters of operations.

As the manuscript lengthened and time wore on, there were things that seemed amiss. Colonel Canham's unclassified top secret missions and the loss of his military papers and records coming home made the story more complex to write, so I decided to write through the eyes of the pilot. Colonel Canham's story provides an insightful picture of the importance of our aircraft and of man during a war conflict and all highly relevant to history.

There's a saying "Thoughts transcends matter." Well, Harry's early thought of wanting to fly proves thoughts can manifest reality. For aviator enthusiasts, it doesn't get any better than to talk with Harry and see the dignity etched on his face in memory of using his God-given gift of flying for the United States Army Air Forces and the United States Air Force. He'll never wave words around. Noble and propounding, Harry grasps the inner significance with understanding and penetration beyond what is superficial or obvious. He has an unmistakable manner about him, poised and graceful in his dress with a deeply ingrained sense of self-discipline.

Harry Canham, an achieved colonel, is a strong believer in paying it forward and helping others toward that goal. He is quick to note any notion that those accomplishments are about him. He was passionate early of what he wanted to do and was optimistic about being a pilot, and with that challenge, he then paid it forward to those cadets who were coming behind him.

May our young men look up to Colonel Canham and those comrades as an example for strength and inspiration. Harry wasn't one to question his ability to function as a pilot; he was answering the call of his country's duty. To Harry, it was a privilege to serve. His outstanding pilot achievement was his brilliant leadership of the United States Army Air Forces and United States Air Force. He contributed immeasurably to the defeat of enemies. Because of his dedication, our hold on the planet was increased. He valued excellence. The Eaker Chapter of the Distinguished Flying Cross Society in Arkansas stated it so well of their member, Col. Harry Canham, "Humble and Gentle in Victory."

Harry's story captures the heart although his modest and unassuming manner resulted in an extremely low profile and lack of awareness of his truly outstanding achievements during his air force years of service. To those that know him, Colonel Canham is a hero; he did his job, incredible and dangerous, all the while flying the skies knowing he may be looking death in the face. Harry proudly has a flag that a light shines upon at night displayed in his yard. It speaks volumes of the love of one's country that he served for thirty-two years, an experience a young Illinois air force pilot will never forget. To retired USAF Col. Harry G. Canham SN40475A, son Michael, brother Morris, and comrades, America owes immeasurable thanks for years of dedication. America shall never forget; without remembrance, there is *no* honor.

Old Glory

Old Glory flies high before him,
Just as he flew his gunship in the skies;
The light shines upon the colors—
Blue and *crimson* and *white* it shines;
With *pride* and *glory* and *honor* he relies.
—Ruby Gwin

Distinguished Flying Cross

Awarded for actions during the Vietnam War

The President of the United States of America, authorized by Act of Congress, July 2, 1926, takes pleasure on presenting the Distinguished Flying Cross to Colonel Harry G. Canham, United States Air Force, for extraordinary achievement while participating in aerial flight as an AC-130 Gunship Pilot over Southeast Asia on 16 January 1972. On that date, while on a night armed reconnaissance mission, his actions led to the damage or destruction of 12 hostile supply vehicles and the ignition of numerous secondary fires and explosions. Putting aside his concern for personal safety in the face of 22 rounds of hostile anti-aircraft fire, he succeeded in destroying large amounts of supplies and munitions destined to use against friendly forces. The professional competence, aerial skill, and devotion to duty displayed by Colonel Canham reflect great credit upon himself and the United States Air Force.

DEPARTMENT OF THE AIR FORCE
OFFICE OF THE CHIEF OF STAFF
UNITED STATES AIR FORCE
WASHINGTON, D.C. 20330

2 8 FEB 1974

Colonel Harry G. Canham
HQ TAC/DO
Langley AFB, Virginia 23665

Dear Colonel Canham

As your active duty years with the United States Air Force come
to an end, I wish to express my sincere appreciation for your
loyal and dedicated service to our country.

During your assignment with the 16th Special Operations Squadron,
Ubon Airfield, Thailand, your professional competence, aerial
skill, and personal devotion to duty aided immeasurably to the
success of the United States Air Force mission in Southeast Asia.
Your actions greatly reduced the capabilities of the enemy and
helped in paving the way for the peace our nation enjoys today.
The many awards you received for that period of combat duty
attest to your outstanding dedication.

As part of the executive management of the Air Force for the past
several years, your many contributions in the operations field
should be a lasting source of pride to you. You will be missed.
I know your interest in the Air Force will continue after you retire.

Again, on behalf of the United States Air Force, I extend my personal
thanks for over three decades of trusted service to your country. It
was a job well done.

Sincerely

GEORGE S. BROWN, General, USAF
Chief of Staff

The Distinguished Flying Cross Society
4442 Vandever Avenue
San Diego, CA 92120-3322

Local	(619) 269-6377		E-mail dfcs@dfcsociety.org
Toll-free	1-866-DFC-MEDAL (332-6332)		www.dfcsociety.org
Fax	(619) 269-6378		

Re: Life Membership

Dear DFCS Member:

Congratulations! You are now a Life Member in good standing in The Distinguished Flying Cross Society. Each Life Member and Regular Member of the DFCS has been awarded the Distinguished Flying Cross, as a result of heroic deeds and extraordinary achievement in aerial flight. Each Associate Member is directly related to one of our Life or Regular Members (i.e. wife, child, or parent). The DFC Society is a registered, non-profit organization with over 4,000 members. All dues and contributions are tax exempt.

Your name has been entered on the DFCS Honor Roll and will remain there in perpetuity. This Honor Roll is maintained by the DFCS Board of Directors in San Diego. Your name has also been placed on our website Honor Roll and can be viewed at www.dfcsociety.org..

The DFCS Board of Directors was elected by the general membership. Its goals are to guide our organization's expansion, recognition and publicity. We are dedicated to the preservation, perpetuation and publication of the history and traditions of those who served in military services worldwide. We are proud and honored to have you as a Life Member of The Distinguished Flying Cross Society. You will be kept up-to-date on our activities by viewing our website periodically, plus we publish a newsletter bi-annually.

If you have any questions, please feel free to e-mail us at dfcs@dfcsociety.org or call toll-free at 1-866-DFC-MEDAL (332-6332).

Welcome Aboard!

Michael E. O'Neil

Michael E. O'Neil
Vice President for Membership

Col. Harry Canham received five Distinguished Flying Crosses.

The first recipient of the Distinguished Flying Cross was Capt. Charles A. Lindbergh for his solo flight across the Atlantic Ocean.

In 1903, the Wright Brothers were awarded Distinguished Flying Cross for their manned flight at Kitty Hawk, North Carolina.

Amelia Earhart is the only female civilian to be awarded the Distinguished Flying Cross by the United States Air Corps for her aerial exploits. Later, such awards were prohibited by an executive order in 1927.

The Military Order of the World Wars

Central Arkansas Chapter #225

Lt Col Thomas A. Robertson, Jr, USAF (Ret.) Commander

Friday, 9 Dec 2011

Col Harry G. Canham, USAF (Ret.)
202 Indianhead Dr
Sherwood, AR 72120-3607

Dear Col Canham,

On behalf of Central Arkansas Chapter Commander, Lt Col Thomas A. Robertson, Jr, USAF (Ret.), and members of our chapter, we thank you and Carlyn for being our luncheon guests at the Jacksonville Western Sizzlin', Wednesday, 7 Dec 2011, and for speaking at the chapter's quarterly meeting. You couldn't have done better. And it was extra special to have so many members of the Ira C. Eaker Chapter, DFC Society with us.

Your career in the USAF was amazing: from staff sergeant glider pilot to B-26, C-46, C-124, F-4, and AC-130. Few could have envisioned the diverse events in which you participated. And Carol said she saw another side of Harry Canham she didn't know: she loved your sense of humor. Nor did I realize you received five DFCs.

Sincerely,

T.P. Williams Col, USAF (Ret.)
Adjutant

cc: Lt Col Thomas A. Robertson, Jr, USAF (Ret.), President
Col Carter Burwell, Jr, USAF (Ret.), AR State Commander
Col James D. Elmer, USAF (Ret.), former CINC, MOWW

314th Airlift Wing
4119 Cannon Drive
Little Rock Air Force Base, Arkansas 72099-5000

Colonel Harry G. Canham, USAF, Retired
Retiree Activities Office
3301 Third Street
Little Rock Air Force Base, Arkansas 72099-5009

Dear Colonel Canham

    I would like to add my congratulations to those of
Major General Porter. Our military retirees are such
an asset to all of us, it is indeed a pleasure to see
a person such as yourself recognized in this way.

    Again, congratulations on this recognition as our
volunteer of the year. Good luck in all your future
endeavors.

               Sincerely

               FREDRIC N. BUCKINGHAM
               Brigadier General, USAF
               Commander

Attachments:
1. Certificate of Appreciation
2. HQ AFMPC/DPMARR Memorandum, 28 Mar 94

cc:
314 SPTG/CC
314 MSSQ/CC

DEPARTMENT OF THE AIR FORCE
HEADQUARTERS AIR FORCE MILITARY PERSONNEL CENTER
RANDOLPH AIR FORCE BASE TEXAS

2 8 MAR 1994

MEMORANDUM FOR 314 AW/CC

FROM: HQ AFMPC/DPMARR
        550 C Street West Ste 11
        Randolph AFB TX 78150-4713

SUBJECT: Retiree Activities Office Recognition Program

    We've enclosed a consolidation of the individual 1993
Retiree Activities Office (RAO) activities reports. We
thought you may be interested in other RAO accomplishments.
We've also included a certificate, signed by Major General
William J. Porter, USAF, Retired, Chairman, Air Force
Retiree Council, for your volunteer of the year. Please
present it at an appropriate ceremony.

    Thank you for your support.

                    CHARLES J. KELLER, GM-14
                    Chief, Retirements Branch
                    Directorate of Pers Prog Mgt

Attachments:
1. RAO Activities Report
2. Certificate - Col Harry G. Canham, USAF, Ret.

11 August 2009

Harry,

On behalf of the Retiree Activities Office volunteers I would like to take this time to thank you for your dedicated service to the United State Air Force and to the retiree population.

Between your service at the Retiree Activities Office and the Little Rock Air Force Base Clinic of almost thirty years service, we thank you.

John S. Heffernan, Director

Harry and son Mike Canham.

Chris and Michelle "Missy" Sergel, Harry, and Carlyn Canham, Father's Day, June 2006, Chicago Hancock Building.

Col. Harry and Carlyn Canham—Harry in military formal attire, 2007.

Harry with prayer afghan throw presented to him by volunteers from the First Methodist Church, Jacksonville, Arkansas. Carlyn is kneeling behind Harry's chair to the right, 2008.

Michael and Gwen Canham in Florida, 6 April 2012.

Harry and Carlyn Canham on Carlyn's birthday, 18 July 2014.

Standing: Michelle Canham Sergel, Father, Mike Canham. *Front:* Samantha Sergel, Harry Canham, and Alex Sergel, June 2012.

Harry Canham with Michelle Sergel, granddaughter, and Alex and Samantha Sergel, great-grandchildren.

(*Standing beside Michael's Learjet 60*) Col. Harry and Carlyn Canham, Gwen and Michael Canham, and Dr. Michelle and Chris Sergel.

Betty, Michael, and Harry Canham with Marc (*standing in the screen door*), 1950.

L-R: Marc Canham (Harry's youngest son, died November 2013) and son, Mathew, and daughter, Marcy. *In front:* Mary Canham.

Marc's daughter, Marcy Canham, Harry's granddaughter, July 7, 2011.

Carlyn with sons (*L-R*) Lee Hinson, Jr., DDS, MAGD (Little Rock, Arkansas) and C. Wallace Hinson, DMA, associate dean, College of Arts and Sciences Piedmont College, Demorest, Georgia, on 18 July 2014 in Little Rock, Arkansas.

L-R: Marsha, Lee, and Katherine Hinson, 18 July 2014.

Alex and Katherine Hinson, son and daughter of R. Lee Hinson, Jr., and Marsha Hinson.

Wallace, "Wally," and Jennifer Hinson, 18 July 2014.

Carlyn feeding the ducks—Harry and Carlyn have a beautiful view out off a lake at the back of their house. Carlyn enjoys feeding the ducks. She will call for them, and they come in for the feeding.

Ducks eating.

Wataga class of 1938 reunion, Bishop Hill, Illinois, 17 June 2006. *L-R:* Col. Harry Canham, Vivian Hammerberg, Dale Johnson, Avis Olson, and (*seated*) Marjorie Olson. Harry and Avis Olson are the only living members of the seventeen class members.

L-R: Neva "Diddy" Fritsche and Carlyn Lilly Canham (sisters). During World War II, Neva was a secretary of a scientist that helped with designing the atomic bomb.

Carolyn Johnson.

Harry Canham and author, Ruby Gwin, in his Sherwood, Arkansas, home October 2014. It was my first meeting with Col. Harry and Carlyn Canham. They were so gracious, and one felt right at home. For daughter, Dr. Deborah Gwin-Hunt, and me, it was most memorable.

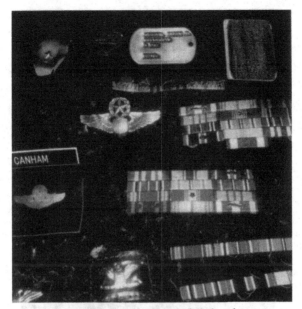

Harry's honorable medal display.

Honorable medals.

Seated: Harry Canham, *standing:* retired pilot, MSgt. Robert "Bob" Davis, and *on right:* Arkansas governor Asa Hutchinson.

Seventy years later, an appreciation day with World War II veterans and their families packed in the State Capitol Rotunda in Little Rock, Arkansas, for the anniversary commemoration of V-J Day of Japan's surrender on 14 August 1945. Harry is recuperating from surgery, but given the military person that he is, no way would he miss such an event. With wife, Carlyn, and help of retired MSgt. Robert B. Davis, Harry was able to attend the V-J Day anniversary. Robert Davis is chapter president of Eaker Distinguish Flying Cross Society.

According to the US Department of Veterans Affairs, there are about eight thousand World War II veterans living in the state of Arkansas. The men and women that fought the great conflict are mostly in their nineties today.

Col. Harry Canham and granddaughter, Dr. Michelle Sergel, 18 July 2014. Michelle in her own pin of the *special* bond with her *granddaddy* Harry Canham:

> *My Grandaddy is one of the most amazing men I have ever met. Until I was in my twenties, I was sure he was a super-human. In my twenties, I got to know him more and know that he is very human . . . not super-human, but that somehow made him more perfect. He ruined me for the rest of the world. To many, he is a war hero . . . undeniably so . . . but he's 'Grandaddy' to me. He's been a guiding light for me since I was a very little girl. My first memory of him was relentlessly following him around the backyard at his home . . . he was so patient and gentle with me. Later, we would talk . . . good long talks. We were adults that could commiserate. He is genuine, hard-working, loyal, so loving . . . and real . . . not many out there that match that. It has been an honor to know my Grandaddy the way I do . . . many granddaughters never do. We have a special closeness. I've trusted him and he's trusted me . . . it is a precious gift that I hold with me forever.*

Michelle Sergel, MD, director of simulation, Cook County Hospital; codirector of simulation, Rush University Simulation Laboratory; assistant professor of Emergency Medicine, Department of Emergency Medicine, Chicago, Illinois.

Harry's granddaughter and Michael Canham's daughter is simulations director Dr. Michelle Sergel, board certified in emergency medicine and internal medicine at Cook County Hospital in Chicago. As one of the founders of the Illinois Medical District Simulation Consortium, she has networked to build a strong collaboration with universities and the Jesse Brown VA Hospital Chicago simulation centers. Dr. Sergel is the president of the Chicago Simulation Consortium. The simulation mannequin is also referred to as *Dummy*. The high fidelity kind simulation can inject medications into and get realistic responses. They have pulses and exhale carbon dioxide. Dr. Sergel travels a lot. She has taken the mannequin to Eastern Europe to Ukraine twice for teaching demonstration, which she found could be comical to take the mannequin through the check-through area. Those at the check-through area had never seen a mannequin. On one of those trips, Customs wouldn't let her through. Dr. Sergel couldn't speak Russian, and doctors had to come out to meet her. Harry said, "I am surprised she doesn't speak Russian because she can do everything else."

At journey's end, Harry had participation in peacetime and during action against an armed enemy that earned him a significant amount of awards for his extended service and campaigns over thirty-two years. Battle stars were awarded for participation in major missions or major campaigns. Harry has left quite an inheritance for history.

Legion of Merit (exceptional meritorious conduct)
World War II Victory Medal
Presidential Unit Citation
Five Distinguished Flying Crosses (heroism) (First one, North Africa, World War II, and four *additional* Flying Crosses, Vietnam, 1972)
Six Meritorious Service Medals
Thirty-two Air Medals (heroic actions or meritorious service in aerial flights)
Armed Forces Reserve Medal
Joint Service Commendation Medal
Air Force Commendations Medal
Combat Readiness Medal—Air Force
Two National Defense Service Medals
Four Vietnam Service Medals (First one, RVN campaign, for outstanding contributions to training and development RVN Armed Forces)
Medal of Honor
American Campaign Medal
Asiatic-Pacific Campaign Medal
European-African-Middle East Campaign Medal
Republic of Vietnam Campaign Medal (Republic of Vietnam)

Harry did not receive a Purple Heart for his mission to deliver a load of ammunition to Vietnam in 1967 when he was seriously injured on 1 August 1967, for it was noted as *peacetime*. The Vietnam War started on 1 November 1955 and ended on Wednesday, 30 April 1975. Colonel Canham flew 22,000 hours during his time served.

Copy of what son Michael had engraved on a large medal cup of aircrafts his father had flown during his thirty-two years in the military.

PT-19AA-26B L-27AF-4D
PT-19BUC-45 C-54EAC-130A
PT-13AC-46A VC-54AC-130E
B-26B C-46D SNBAC-130H
B-26CAT-6CT-28
B-26G AT-6DC-119
L-4 B AT-11 T-29A
UC-78 T-7 T-29B
C-47A T-11 T-29D
C-47D C-74EC-135
B-25H B-17G EC-145
A-20HC-124AC-130B
C-49T-33A C-130E

Printed in the United States
By Bookmasters